The Politics of Climate

Other Books of Related Interest

Opposing Viewpoints Series
America's Infrastructure and the Green Economy
Government Gridlock
Green Politics

At Issue Series
The Media's Influence on Society
Pipelines and Politics
The Role of Science in Public Policy

Current Controversies Series
Climate Change and Biodiversity
Fossil Fuel Industries and the Green Economy
Sustainable Consumption

> "Congress shall make no law ... abridging the freedom of speech, or of the press."
>
> *First Amendment to the U.S. Constitution*

The basic foundation of our democracy is the First Amendment guarantee of freedom of expression. The Opposing Viewpoints series is dedicated to the concept of this basic freedom and the idea that it is more important to practice it than to enshrine it.

The Politics of Climate

Avery Elizabeth Hurt, Book Editor

Published in 2023 by Greenhaven Publishing, LLC
2544 Clinton Street,
Buffalo NY 14224

Copyright © 2024 by Greenhaven Publishing, LLC

First Edition

All rights reserved. No part of this book may be reproduced in any form without permission in writing from the publisher, except by a reviewer.

Articles in Greenhaven Publishing anthologies are often edited for length to meet page requirements. In addition, original titles of these works are changed to clearly present the main thesis and to explicitly indicate the author's opinion. Every effort is made to ensure that Greenhaven Publishing accurately reflects the original intent of the authors. Every effort has been made to trace the owners of the copyrighted material.

Cover image: Scott Book/Shutterstock.com

Library of Congress CataloginginPublication Data

Names: Hurt, Avery Elizabeth, editor.
Title: The politics of climate / edited by Avery Elizabeth Hurt.
Description: First Edition. | New York : Greenhaven Publishing, 2024. | Series: Opposing viewpoints | Includes bibliographic references and index.
Identifiers: ISBN 9781534509337 (pbk.) | ISBN 9781534509344 (library bound)
Subjects: LCSH: Climatic changes--Juvenile literature. | Climatic changes--Effect of human beings on--Juvenile literature. | Climatic changes--Social aspects--Juvenile literature. | Climatic changes--Political aspects--Juvenile literature. | Climatic changes--Government policy--Juvenile literature. | Global environmental change--Juvenile literature.
Classification: LCC QC903.15 P655 2024 | DDC 304.2'5--dc23

Manufactured in the United States of America

Website: http://greenhavenpublishing.com

Contents

The Importance of Opposing Viewpoints	11
Introduction	14

Chapter 1: Are Today's Political Systems Ill-Equipped to Deal with Climate Change?

Chapter Preface	18
1. The U.S. Political System Makes It Hard to Pass Climate Change Legislation *Amy Scott and Richard Cunningham*	19
2. The U.S.'s Climate Bill Is Historic, but It Doesn't Get Everything Right *Alice C. Hill and Madeline Babin*	24
3. We Need to Make Democracy Work for Long-Term Solutions to Climate Change *Roman Krznaric*	29
4. Government Failure to Act Isn't the Main Barrier to Climate Action *Nick Bernards*	36
5. The Supreme Court Creates a New Obstacle for Climate Action *Michael Gerrard*	41
Periodical and Internet Sources Bibliography	45

Chapter 2: Who Should Pay for the Impacts of Climate Change?

Chapter Preface	48
1. Climate Change Brings Ethical Responsibilities *William S. Lynn*	49
2. Rich, Polluting Countries Owe the Developing World *Courtney Lindwall*	56

3. Wealthy Nations Are Reluctant to Financially Commit to Helping Developing Nations Affected by Climate Change — 62
Lauren Sommer

4. Rich Countries Need to Get Serious and Specific About Climate Finance — 68
Rishikesh Ram Bhandary

5. The Focus of Climate Finance and Justice Needs to Shift from Countries to Individuals — 73
John Vogler and Marit Hammond

6. Carbon Taxes Can Work — 77
Gilbert E. Metcalf

7. The International Court of Justice Could Advise on What Countries Owe for Their Roles in Climate Change — 82
Jacqueline Peel and Zoe Nay

Periodical and Internet Sources Bibliography — 87

Chapter 3: Has the Media Made Climate Change More Politically Polarizing?

Chapter Preface — 90

1. The Media Has Covered Climate Change for More than 100 Years — 91
Linden Ashcroft

2. The Media Gets Climate Change Wrong — 97
Stephan Lewandowsky and Michael Ashley

3. Climate Change Misinformation Fools Too Many People — 104
Mikey Biddlestone and Sander van der Linden

4. Climate Misinformation on Social Media Is Undermining Climate Action — 109
Jeff Turrentine

5. Changing the Language Used in Climate Coverage Can Help the Media Reach Climate Skeptics — 116
Denise-Marie Ordway

6. News Stories on Climate Change Need to Offer
   a More Optimistic Message **123**
   Jon Christensen

Periodical and Internet Sources Bibliography **129**

Chapter 4: Should Climate Change Be Addressed as a Local Issue?

Chapter Preface **132**

1. We Need Powerful, Local Stories to Inspire Action
   on Climate Change **133**
   Kamyar Razavi

2. Individual Choices Make a Difference in Fighting
   Climate Change **139**
   Tom Ptak

3. Connect, Bond, and Inspire for Effective Climate
   Conversations **144**
   Aven Frey

4. When Talking About Climate Change, Speak Like
   the Locals **149**
   Jason Mark

5. Cities Are Both a Cause of and Solution to
   Climate Change **153**
   United Nations

6. Reducing Climate Action to Individual Choices
   Has a Harmful Effect **158**
   Taha Yasseri and Mary Sanford

Periodical and Internet Sources Bibliography **162**

For Further Discussion **164**
Organizations to Contact **167**
Bibliography of Books **171**
Index **173**

The Importance of Opposing Viewpoints

Perhaps every generation experiences a period in time in which the populace seems especially polarized, starkly divided on the important issues of the day and gravitating toward the far ends of the political spectrum and away from a consensus-facilitating middle ground. The world that today's students are growing up in and that they will soon enter into as active and engaged citizens is deeply fragmented in just this way. Issues relating to terrorism, immigration, women's rights, minority rights, race relations, health care, taxation, wealth and poverty, the environment, policing, military intervention, the proper role of government—in some ways, perennial issues that are freshly and uniquely urgent and vital with each new generation—are currently roiling the world.

If we are to foster a knowledgeable, responsible, active, and engaged citizenry among today's youth, we must provide them with the intellectual, interpretive, and critical-thinking tools and experience necessary to make sense of the world around them and of the all-important debates and arguments that inform it. After all, the outcome of these debates will in large measure determine the future course, prospects, and outcomes of the world and its peoples, particularly its youth. If they are to become successful members of society and productive and informed citizens, students need to learn how to evaluate the strengths and weaknesses of someone else's arguments, how to sift fact from opinion and fallacy, and how to test the relative merits and validity of their own opinions against the known facts and the best possible available information. The landmark series Opposing Viewpoints has been providing students with just such critical-thinking skills and exposure to the debates surrounding society's most urgent contemporary issues for many years, and it continues to serve this essential role with undiminished commitment, care, and rigor.

The key to the series's success in achieving its goal of sharpening students' critical-thinking and analytic skills resides in its title—

Opposing Viewpoints. In every intriguing, compelling, and engaging volume of this series, readers are presented with the widest possible spectrum of distinct viewpoints, expert opinions, and informed argumentation and commentary, supplied by some of today's leading academics, thinkers, analysts, politicians, policy makers, economists, activists, change agents, and advocates. Every opinion and argument anthologized here is presented objectively and accorded respect. There is no editorializing in any introductory text or in the arrangement and order of the pieces. No piece is included as a "straw man," an easy ideological target for cheap point-scoring. As wide and inclusive a range of viewpoints as possible is offered, with no privileging of one particular political ideology or cultural perspective over another. It is left to each individual reader to evaluate the relative merits of each argument—as he or she sees it, and with the use of ever-growing critical-thinking skills—and grapple with his or her own assumptions, beliefs, and perspectives to determine how convincing or successful any given argument is and how the reader's own stance on the issue may be modified or altered in response to it.

This process is facilitated and supported by volume, chapter, and selection introductions that provide readers with the essential context they need to begin engaging with the spotlighted issues, with the debates surrounding them, and with their own perhaps shifting or nascent opinions on them. In addition, guided reading and discussion questions encourage readers to determine the authors' point of view and purpose, interrogate and analyze the various arguments and their rhetoric and structure, evaluate the arguments' strengths and weaknesses, test their claims against available facts and evidence, judge the validity of the reasoning, and bring into clearer, sharper focus the reader's own beliefs and conclusions and how they may differ from or align with those in the collection or those of their classmates.

Research has shown that reading comprehension skills improve dramatically when students are provided with compelling, intriguing, and relevant "discussable" texts. The subject matter of these collections could not be more compelling, intriguing, or urgently relevant to today's students and the world they are poised to inherit. The anthologized articles and the reading and discussion questions that are included with them also provide the basis for stimulating, lively, and passionate classroom debates. Students who are compelled to anticipate objections to their own argument and identify the flaws in those of an opponent read more carefully, think more critically, and steep themselves in relevant context, facts, and information more thoroughly. In short, using discussable text of the kind provided by every single volume in the Opposing Viewpoints series encourages close reading, facilitates reading comprehension, fosters research, strengthens critical thinking, and greatly enlivens and energizes classroom discussion and participation. The entire learning process is deepened, extended, and strengthened.

For all of these reasons, Opposing Viewpoints continues to be exactly the right resource at exactly the right time—when we most need to provide readers with the critical-thinking tools and skills that will not only serve them well in school but also in their careers and their daily lives as decision-making family members, community members, and citizens. This series encourages respectful engagement with and analysis of opposing viewpoints and fosters a resulting increase in the strength and rigor of one's own opinions and stances. As such, it helps make readers "future ready," and that readiness will pay rich dividends for the readers themselves, for the citizenry, for our society, and for the world at large.

Introduction

> "We're standing at an inflection point in world history. Cleaner air for our children. More bountiful oceans. Healthier forests and ecosystems for our planet. We can create an environment that raises the standard of living around the world. And this is a moral imperative, but this is also an economic imperative."
>
> —U.S. President Joe Biden

In a 2022 article in the *New Yorker*, journalist Elizabeth Kolbert tells the story of an event on the U.S. presidential campaign trail in 2000. A climate activist, dressed in a red cape and yellow galoshes and calling himself Captain Climate, approached any candidate he could get close to and shouted, "What's your climate plan?" Only one candidate out of a field of more than a dozen bothered to answer him. That was John McCain, a Republican senator from Arizona at that time. Later McCain would introduce a bill to limit carbon dioxide emissions. It did not pass, but Kolbert tells us that McCain responded to the failure to pass the legislation by saying, "We've lost a big battle today, but we'll win over time, because climate change is real."[1]

If you've been reading the papers or watching the news in recent years, that story may seem unbelievable. But the fact is, climate change has not always been a political issue. More than 20 years ago, when Captain Climate was needling candidates about their climate plans, the issue of global warming was an environmental issue, a scientific issue. It was not partisan, for it was as obvious

Introduction

then as it is now that the climate has no party registration; the devastation brought about by climate change will affect everyone, no matter their political views. When bills like Senator McCain's failed to pass, it was not because people thought—as many do now, according to sources quoted in this volume—that climate change is part of a "leftwing agenda." It was more a matter of not being able to reach agreement on what should be done about it.

As early as 2000, Captain Climate and others were sounding the alarm for a distressed planet. Even so, 22 years would go by before Congress passed major climate legislation. When the Inflation Reduction Act was passed in 2022 with the intention of fueling the U.S.'s clean energy transition and mitigating the effects of climate change, that legislation was passed along party lines.[2] In the intervening years since Captain Climate called out politicians, the issue of climate change has become increasingly political, particularly in the United States and other English-speaking nations. That is beginning to change, however, as increasing numbers of citizens say they're concerned about climate change.

In *Opposing Viewpoints: The Politics of Climate*, viewpoint authors from a wide variety of backgrounds take a close look at the politics of climate change: what has changed, what hasn't, and how those who are concerned about the effects of climate change are trying to talk with those who don't understand the problem or don't believe it's happening. In Chapter 1, entitled "Are Today's Political Systems Ill-Equipped to Deal with Climate Change?", the viewpoints focus mainly on the climate bill that eventually passed in 2022—the Inflation Reduction Act (IRA), so named because the money it authorizes to address climate change is also expected to boost the economy.

The authors in Chapter 2—"Who Should Pay for the Impacts of Climate Change?"—ask if climate change is a social justice and ethical issue, and if so, what should be done to fairly distribute the costs of preparing for and repairing the damage from disasters caused by climate change. Chapter 3—"Has the Media Made Climate Change More Politically Polarizing?"—features viewpoints that examine the media's role in making climate change a political issue. Have journalists done an adequate job of informing and educating the public about this crucial issue? If not, how can they improve?

In the final chapter entitled "Should Climate Change Be Addressed as a Local Issue?", the authors look at climate change as an issue that can potentially be addressed by smaller communities. The effects, after all, are felt by people in communities, not abstractly. Here, several of the authors address how we might be able to reduce the politics and increase the civility of the conversation, both in our families and in our communities, by listening to each other and sharing our views respectfully. The viewpoints in *Opposing Viewpoints: The Politics of Climate* explore this urgent issue from a wide variety of angles and offer potential solutions for depolarizing the politics of climate.

Notes

1. Elizabeth Kolbert, "How Did Fighting Climate Change Become a Partisan Issue?" *New Yorker,* August 14, 2022. https://www.newyorker.com/magazine/2022/08/22/how-did-fighting-climate-change-become-a-partisan-issue.
2. Ella Nilsen, "Republicans Voted 'No' on the Climate Bill. Their States Will Get Billions of Dollars from It Anyway," CNN, August 31, 2022. https://www.cnn.com/2022/08/31/politics/republican-states-benefit-climate-law/index.html.

CHAPTER 1

Are Today's Political Systems Ill-Equipped to Deal with Climate Change?

Chapter Preface

Until the 2022 passage of the Inflation Reduction Act (abbreviated the IRA and often called "the climate bill" because it's primarily a package of economic spending and incentives intended to mitigate climate change), the United States seemed incapable of taking any serious steps to address the problem. Many people say the IRA is not enough and fear that subsequent administrations and Congresses will act to weaken it.

Climate change has not always been a political issue. As we saw in the introduction, only a few decades ago, there was large consensus among Americans about the importance of environmental responsibility and environmental justice. Today that has changed. Thanks at least in part to the powerful lobbying and public relations efforts of companies whose business models contribute to climate change, the public is divided about the issue, largely along party lines.

However, party politics are not the only problem. The very nature of democracy makes it difficult to address long-term problems. And climate change is certainly a long-term problem. Frequent election cycles mean politicians often focus on immediate issues and suggest responses that can be enacted immediately. No politician wants their successor to get credit for hard work they did. In addition, politicians are often beholden to financial backers whose interests are quite different from the interests of the public and the environment in which citizens and their children and grandchildren will live. This short-term focus neglects many long-term issues. Climate change is one of them.

This chapter opens with a viewpoint examining how climate change became a political issue. Then there are several takes on the climate bill—what it achieved and where it missed the mark. Experts also consider why democracy isn't good at dealing with long-term problems and offers suggestions for re-inventing democracy so that it can better serve the interests of the future.

VIEWPOINT 1

> "Congress doesn't have a great track record in passing climate legislation—the United States ranked 28th in the world for climate protection measures, according to the Climate Change Performance Index."

The U.S. Political System Makes It Hard to Pass Climate Change Legislation

Amy Scott and Richard Cunningham

Although later in 2022, after this viewpoint was published in January, Congress did pass a massive bill (the Inflation Reduction Act) that contained much of President Biden's climate agenda, at the time this viewpoint was originally published no major climate-related legislation had passed through Congress. However, in this viewpoint—an interview with Shannon Osaka, a reporter from Grist, and Amy Scott—Scott and Osaka dig into why the U.S. political system makes it easier to block change than the create it. Amy Scott is a host of the public radio program "Marketplace," and Richard Cunningham is an associate producer there.

As you read, consider the following questions:

1. West Virginia has a pattern of blocking action on climate change. Why?

"Why It's So Hard to Pass Climate Crisis Legislation in the U.S.," by Amy Scott and Richard Cunningham, Marketplace, January 27, 2022. Reprinted by permission.

2. What does Osaka mean by "double representation"? How can this lead to a less effective Congress?
3. Why would "one more seat in Senate" change the situation dramatically, according to Osaka?

In December, Democratic Sen. Joe Manchin of West Virginia said he "cannot vote to continue with" the Build Back Better Act, stalling President Joe Biden's massive social spending bill. The sweeping $1.7 trillion bill includes provisions for health care, affordable housing, universal pre-K and climate investments. But there's hope that the climate investment portion can be passed separately in a $500 billion agreement.

Congress doesn't have a great track record in passing climate legislation—the United States ranked 28th in the world for climate protection measures, according to the Climate Change Performance Index. Policy failures from the last three decades include President Bill Clinton's proposed carbon-dioxide tax and President Barack Obama's cap-and-trade proposal. Many blame the growing polarization in American politics.

But Shannon Osaka, a reporter from Grist, has a different perspective. In a recent article, she argues that the problem is a fundamental issue with American democracy, because in our political system, it's much easier to block change than it is to create it. "Marketplace" host Amy Scott sat down to discuss the latest in the Build Back Better plan and why our political system makes it hard to pass climate laws.

The following is an edited transcript of their conversation.

Amy Scott: What climate policies are at stake in the president's Build Back Better agenda? And what would they accomplish if some version of this doesn't end up passing?

Shannon Osaka: I mean, the Build Back Better plan for climate is just huge. It's about $500 billion toward clean energy. We're talking things like tax credits for electric vehicles, for building geothermal, solar and wind power plants. And if this passes, I mean, it will be the biggest climate plan that the U.S. has ever put through Congress. And it will get us much closer on a path to cutting our carbon emissions in line with the Paris Agreement.

Scott: Now, this isn't the first time that a Democratic senator from West Virginia has blocked a Democratic president's climate plan. Talk about what happened back in 1993.

Osaka: Yeah, so it's a pretty crazy history. So effectively, when Bill Clinton was president, he wanted to put through basically what would be a carbon tax, so a tax on carbon dioxide emissions. And it was blocked by the senator named Robert Byrd who was from West Virginia. And he basically said, "I don't support a carbon tax, because, you know, we have a lot of fossil fuels in West Virginia. It doesn't suit my constituents." So the Clinton administration had to try a different tack, and their other backup plan also failed. And so this is just a sign of how in the U.S., we've been trying to pass climate policy for such a long time and we just keep getting stuck.

Scott: And often it comes down to one vote or relatively small obstacle, right? In your article, you write about so many times that we could have taken steps that we didn't.

Osaka: Right, and it's very interesting, because if we think about the United States, just as you know, an example of a country that's really struggled to pass climate policy, there are certain sort of structural things about the U.S. that make it really difficult. If you think about being in sort of, you know, middle school civics class, they talk about separation of powers, and separation of powers can be great for a lot of things. But it also means that there's lots of opportunities to block change, and I think what we've seen in the U.S. over the past 20-30 years has been a lot of using that separation of powers to prevent climate policy from passing.

Climate Division Runs Deep

Political fissures on climate issues extend far beyond beliefs about whether climate change is occurring and whether humans are playing a role, according to a new, in-depth survey by Pew Research Center. These divisions reach across every dimension of the climate debate, down to people's basic trust in the motivations that drive climate scientists to conduct their research.

Specifically, the survey finds wide political divides in views of the potential for devastation to the Earth's ecosystems and what might be done to address any climate impacts. There are also major divides in the way partisans interpret the current scientific discussion over climate, with the political left and right having vastly divergent perceptions of modern scientific consensus, differing levels of trust in the information they get from professional researchers, and different views as to whether it is the quest for knowledge or the quest for professional advancement that drives climate scientists in their work.

At the same time, political differences are not the exclusive drivers of people's views about climate issues. People's level of concern about the issue also matters. The 36% of Americans who are more personally concerned about the issue of global climate change, whether they are Republican or Democrat, are much more likely to see climate science as settled, to believe that humans are playing a role in causing the Earth to warm, and to put great faith in climate scientists.

"The Politics of Climate", Pew Research Center, October 4, 2016.

Scott: You also mentioned this term "double representation" to talk about the role that corporations play in this inability to pass climate policy. Can you explain that?

Osaka: Yeah, so double representation is this really interesting term that was coined by this political scientist named Matto Mildenberger. And he basically says that fossil fuel interests are represented on both sides of the aisle. So they're represented on the left through labor unions and industrial workers. And on the right, they're represented through corporations and business interests. So in some ways, you could say, "OK, well, maybe that's going to be good because that means that there's also climate supporters on both sides of the aisle." But in practice, in a system like the United States where we have so many veto points, what happens is that there's lots of opportunities for actors on both sides of the aisle to stop change.

Scott: It seems that, you know, given this history of the failure of climate policy in Congress, you're actually still hopeful that the U.S. can lead on climate policy. Why is that?

Osaka: Well, I think that when you look at the history, we've been so close so many times. I mean, there's all of these moments where things really could have gone a different way. And, I mean, if you look at the situation now, if Democrats had just one more seat in the Senate, you and I might be having a totally different conversation. We might be talking about, "Oh, the Build Back Better Act just passed. Here's all the things that are in it for climate." So there's this level of sort of randomness or stochasticity that comes in, that means that, you know, we kind of just need everything to line up in the right way. And over the past 20 years, it hasn't. But that doesn't mean that it can't. And I think that, you know, when we're talking about the majority of people supporting climate policy and really wanting the U.S. to act, I think that that is just going to get stronger and stronger as we move through time. And I just hope that we act before it's too late.

VIEWPOINT

> "Because the IRA has a decade-long timespan, the risk remains that changes in administration could slow climate investment. Still, since this is a congressional act—not an executive order—it will require legislative or judicial action to undo, thus making it harder to reverse."

The U.S.'s Climate Bill Is Historic, but It Doesn't Get Everything Right

Alice C. Hill and Madeline Babin

In the previous viewpoint, Amy Scott and Shannon Osaka expressed the hope that the U.S. would pass major climate legislation. Later that year, in August of 2022, President Biden signed legislation that included a $370 billion investment in climate action. In this viewpoint, Alice C. Hill and Madeline Babin answer common questions about the bill and point out ways in which it could have been improved. Alice Hill is senior fellow for energy and the environment at the Council on Foreign Relations (CFR), and Madeline Babin is a research associate in climate change policy for the CFR.

"What the Historic U.S. Climate Bill Gets Right and Gets Wrong", by Alice C. Hill, CFR Expert and Madeline Babin, Council on Foreign Relations, August 17, 2022. Reprinted by permission.

As you read, consider the following questions:

1. As explained in this viewpoint, what is the difference between emissions-cutting technologies and resilience technologies?
2. These authors say the bill falls short of the administration's initial targets, but that it enables other factors that could "bridge the gap." What are those factors?
3. What problems do the authors have with the bill?

The Inflation Reduction Act promises the largest investment in climate action in U.S. history—$370 billion—and could lead to significant emissions reductions over the next decade.

Q: What major climate action is included in the Inflation Reduction Act (IRA)?

A: The Inflation Reduction Act of 2022, approved by Congress and signed by President Joe Biden in August, is set to deliver the largest investment in climate action in U.S. history. Congress has directed nearly $370 billion over the next decade to rapidly scale up renewable energy production and drive substantial reductions in greenhouse gas emissions.

The historic legislation invests in a variety of efforts, including low-carbon technologies, environmental justice initiatives for disadvantaged communities, and tax credits to promote electric vehicle sales. The IRA pours $27 billion into creating a green bank to finance clean energy technologies and emission-cutting infrastructure, such as residential rooftop solar panels. Billions more go to climate-smart agricultural practices and clean-vehicle manufacturing facilities. Additional funding for consumer programs—including those that underwrite the use of heat pumps, which are energy-saving systems that help regulate home temperatures—will improve home energy efficiency. The IRA also directs $1.5 billion to reduce methane leaks from natural gas production to support the U.S. commitment to the Global Methane Pledge.

On the resilience side, Congress will hand out $5 billion in grants to support fire-resilient forests, forest conservation, and urban tree planting. The bill also allocates several billion dollars in funding for drought resilience in western states.

Q: What doesn't it include?

A: The bill focuses heavily on emission-cutting solutions to climate change and mostly neglects resilience.

In its aim to make buildings more energy efficient, it misses an opportunity to make sure buildings will withstand the climate-fueled extremes that the nation is already experiencing and will continue to endure. Last year, climate events inflicted more than $152 billion in damages across the country, and this year, climate change has brought flash flooding in California, Kentucky, and Montana as well as wildfires in Alaska, California, and New Mexico. The National Oceanic and Atmospheric Administration (NOAA) predicts increased hurricane activity in the coming months. When communities rebuild after disasters, they risk restoring structures doomed to fail in the next catastrophe, since the United States lacks climate-resilient building codes.

Q: What are other concerns about the bill?

A: Some measures included in the IRA could inadvertently harm U.S. climate efforts. For example, the bill includes a clean hydrogen tax credit, which is intended to help drive down the cost of hydrogen production. However, recent findings* have cast doubt on hydrogen's role in a clean energy future. Scientists have found that hydrogen, which is prone to leaking, contributes to global heating when it escapes into the atmosphere. Using hydrogen to tackle climate change will require effective monitoring of leaks, but current technology only detects amounts high enough to cause explosions.

The legislation also includes a provision that tethers offshore wind leasing to oil and gas extraction. Over a ten-year period, the Interior Department will be prohibited from issuing a lease for offshore wind development unless at least 60 million acres—the size of Michigan—have been leased for oil and gas in the previous year. The bill also requires that the Interior Department offer to lease** at least two million acres of public lands—more than double the size of Rhode Island—for oil and gas drilling as a prerequisite for any renewable energy development on public lands. Experts, such as the Center for Biological Diversity's Brett Hartl, have voiced concern that "handcuffing" renewable energy development to new oil and gas extraction will "fan the flames of climate disasters torching our country."

Q: Will the legislation lead to meaningful reductions of greenhouse gas emissions?

A: Analysts predict that the IRA will result in a 41 percent reduction in U.S. emissions by 2030, compared to 2005 levels. While this would be an improvement from the projected 27 percent reduction that would have happened regardless of the bill's passage, it falls short of the Biden administration's commitment to reduce emissions by at least 50 percent from 2005 levels by 2030.

However, additional federal regulatory action or increased state and local climate efforts could make up the difference. And the bill's provisions that lower clean energy costs and incentivize investment in renewables will alleviate some of the barriers that have deterred state and local action, which could galvanize the efforts needed to bridge the gap.

Q: Will it improve the United States' global image?

A: The IRA will go a long way toward restoring the United States' credibility as a global leader on climate. As the largest emitter historically and the second-largest emitter currently, the United

States faces skepticism as it urges other nations to act on climate. By effectively demonstrating a plan to fulfill climate commitments, the IRA will strengthen U.S. legitimacy in international climate negotiations when nations convene in November for the 27th Conference of the Parties (COP27).

While setbacks to the administration's climate agenda have "slowed the pace" of other countries' emissions-reduction efforts, as U.S. climate envoy John Kerry has said, the United States' passage of the biggest climate legislation in its history could inspire other countries to take action to avoid falling behind.

Q: Are there any challenges to rolling out the legislation?

A: Because the IRA has a decade-long timespan, the risk remains that changes in administration could slow climate investment. Still, since this is a congressional act—not an executive order—it will require legislative or judicial action to undo, thus making it harder to reverse. In addition, courts will likely be less sympathetic to any claims that federal rulemaking pursuant to the bill violates the major questions doctrine recently articulated by the Supreme Court in *West Virginia v. Environmental Protection Agency (EPA)*.

Ensuring that the IRA's funding goes to initiatives that actually help combat climate change will pose a challenge. For example, though the bill allocates billions of dollars to support climate-smart agriculture, critics have warned that some of the targeted programs could do more harm than good by funding projects that increase emissions by incentivizing land clearing, fertilizer use, and intensive animal breeding.

*Editor's note: Author Alice C. Hill is on the board of the Environmental Defense Fund, which produced this report.
**Editor's note: The legislation only requires that land be offered for leasing, not that it actually be leased.

Viewpoint

> *"Nations bicker around international conference tables, focused on their near-term interests, while the planet burns and species disappear."*

We Need to Make Democracy Work for Long-Term Solutions to Climate Change

Roman Krznaric

Most of the viewpoints in this chapter have focused on the Inflation Reduction Act, also known as the climate bill. It's a good example of democracy getting something done about climate change. In this viewpoint, Roman Krznaric looks at the particular difficulties democracies have in addressing long-term problems such as climate change. The answer is not to replace democracy with "benign dictators," he says, but to reinvent democracy itself. According to the author, representative democracy consistently tends to focus on present-day concerns over the issues that today's actions will have on future generations. By shifting the focus from the here-and-now, democracies will be better equipped to meaningfully address the challenges of climate change. Roman Krznaric is an Australian philosopher and political scientist.

As you read, consider the following questions:

1. Why do governments generally prefer "quick fixes?"

"Why we need to reinvent democracy for the long-term," by Roman Krznaric, BBC, March 19, 2019. Reprinted by permission.

2. How do corporations take advantage of the electoral cycle to reap benefits for themselves at the expense of the public?
3. What does Krznaric mean when he says we have colonized the future?

"The origin of civil government," wrote David Hume in 1739, is that "men are not able radically to cure, either in themselves or others, that narrowness of soul, which makes them prefer the present to the remote." The Scottish philosopher was convinced that the institutions of government—such as political representatives and parliamentary debates—would serve to temper our impulsive and selfish desires, and foster society's long-term interests and welfare.

Today Hume's view appears little more than wishful thinking, since it is so startlingly clear that our political systems have become a cause of rampant short-termism rather than a cure for it. Many politicians can barely see beyond the next election, and dance to the tune of the latest opinion poll or tweet. Governments typically prefer quick fixes, such as putting more criminals behind bars rather than dealing with the deeper social and economic causes of crime. Nations bicker around international conference tables, focused on their near-term interests, while the planet burns and species disappear.

As the 24/7 news media pumps out the latest twist in the Brexit negotiations or obsesses over a throwaway comment from the U.S. president, the myopia of modern democratic politics is all too obvious. So is there an antidote to this political presentism that pushes the interests of future generations permanently beyond the horizon?

Let's start with the nature of the problem. It's common to claim that today's short-termism is simply a product of social media and other digital technologies that have ratcheted up the pace of political life. But the fixation on the now has far deeper roots.

Are Today's Political Systems Ill-Equipped to Deal with Climate Change?

One problem is the electoral cycle, an inherent design flaw of democratic systems that produces short political time horizons. Politicians might offer enticing tax breaks to woo voters at the next electoral contest, while ignoring long-term issues out of which they can make little immediate political capital, such as dealing with ecological breakdown, pension reform or investing in early childhood education. Back in the 1970s, this form of myopic policy-making was dubbed the "political business cycle."

Add to this the ability of special interest groups—especially corporations—to use the political system to secure near-term benefits for themselves while passing the longer-term costs onto the rest of society. Whether through the funding of electoral campaigns or big-budget lobbying, the corporate hacking of politics is a global phenomenon that pushes long-term policy making off the agenda.

The third and deepest cause of political presentism is that representative democracy systematically ignores the interests of future people. The citizens of tomorrow are granted no rights, nor—in the vast majority of countries—are there any bodies to represent their concerns or potential views on decisions today that will undoubtedly affect their lives. It's a blind spot so enormous that we barely notice it: in the decade I spent as a political scientist specialising in democratic governance, it simply never occurred to me that future generations are disenfranchised in the same way that slaves or women were in the past. But that is the reality. And that's why hundreds of thousands of schoolchildren worldwide, inspired by Swedish teenager Greta Thunberg, have been striking and marching to get rich nations to reduce their carbon emissions: they have had enough of democratic systems that render them voiceless and airbrush their futures out of the political picture.

The time has come to face an inconvenient reality: that modern democracy—especially in wealthy countries—has enabled us to colonise the future. We treat the future like a distant colonial outpost devoid of people, where we can freely dump ecological degradation, technological risk, nuclear waste and public debt, and that we feel at liberty to plunder as we please. When Britain colonized Australia in the 18th and 19th century, it drew on the legal doctrine now known as terra nullius—nobody's land—to justify its conquest and treat the indigenous population as if they didn't exist or have any claims on the land. Today our attitude is one of tempus nullius. The future is an "empty time," an unclaimed territory that is similarly devoid of inhabitants. Like the distant realms of empire, it is ours for the taking.

The daunting challenge we face is to reinvent democracy itself to overcome its inherent short-termism and to address the intergenerational theft that underlies our colonial domination of the future. How to do so is, I believe, the most urgent political challenge of our times.

Some suggest that democracy is so fundamentally short-sighted that we might be better off with "benign dictators," who can take the long view on the multiple crises facing humanity on behalf of us all. Amongst them is the eminent British astronomer Martin Rees, who has written that on critical long-term challenges such as climate change and the spread of bioweapons, "only an enlightened despot could push through the measures needed to navigate the 21st century safely." When I recently asked him in a public forum whether he was offering dictatorship as a serious policy prescription to deal with short-termism, and suggested that perhaps he had been joking, he replied, "actually, I was semi-serious." He then gave the example of China as an authoritarian regime that was incredibly successful at long-term planning, evident in its huge ongoing investment in solar power.

A surprisingly large number of heads were nodding in the audience, but mine was not amongst them. History has few, if any, examples of dictators who remain benign and enlightened for very long (witness, for instance, China's record on human rights). Moreover, there is little evidence that authoritarian regimes have a better record on long-term thinking and planning than democratic ones: Sweden, for instance, manages to generate almost 60% of its electricity through renewables without having a despot in charge (compared to only 26% in China).

A more fundamental point is that there may be ways to reinvent representative democracy to overcome its current bias towards the here and now. In fact, several countries have already embarked on pioneering experiments to empower the citizens of the future. Finland, for instance, has a parliamentary Committee for the Future that scrutinizes legislation for its impact on future generations. Between 2001 and 2006 Israel had an Ombudsman for Future Generations, although the position was abolished as it was deemed to have too much power to delay legislation.

Perhaps the best-known contemporary example is in Wales, which established a Future Generations Commissioner, Sophie Howe, as part of the 2015 Well-being for Future Generations Act. The role of the commissioner is to ensure that public bodies in Wales working in areas ranging from environmental protection to employment schemes, make policy decisions looking at least 30 years into the future. There are now growing calls for a similar Future Generations Act to cover the whole U.K. It's an idea that may gain traction with a new All-Party Parliamentary Group for Future Generations, formed in 2018 with support from Martin Rees, who sits in the House of Lords and clearly still has some faith in the democratic process.

Such initiatives have been criticised, however, for being too reformist and doing little to alter the structure of democratic government at a fundamental level. A more radical alternative has been suggested by the veteran Canadian ecological campaigner David Suzuki, who wants to replace the country's elected politicians with a randomly selected citizens' assembly, which would contain everyday Canadians with no party affiliation who would each spend six years in office. In his view, such an assembly, resembling a form of political jury service, would deal more effectively with long-term issues such as climate change and biodiversity loss, and solve the problem of politicians obsessed with the next election.

But could an assembly of today's citizens really be able to step into the shoes of future generations and effectively represent their interests? A new movement in Japan called Future Design is attempting to answer this very question. Led by economist Tatsuyoshi Saijo of the Research Institute for Humanity and Nature in Kyoto, the movement has been conducting citizen assemblies in municipalities across the country. One group of participants takes the position of current residents, and the other group imagines themselves to be "future residents" from the year 2060, even wearing special ceremonial robes to aid their imaginative leap forward in time. Multiple studies have shown that the future residents devise far more radical and progressive city plans compared to current ones. Ultimately the movement aims to establish a Ministry of the Future as part of central government, and a Department of the Future within all local government authorities, which would use the future citizens' assembly model for policy-making.

Future Design is partly inspired by the Seventh Generation Principle, observed by some Native American peoples, where the impact on the welfare of the seventh generation in the future (around 150 years ahead) is taken into account.

Such indigenous thinking has also motivated a major lawsuit in the U.S., where the youth-led organisation Our Children's Trust is attempting to secure the legal right to a stable climate and healthy atmosphere for the benefit of all present and future generations. What makes this case notable is that the plaintiffs are in their teens or early 20s. They are arguing the U.S. government has wittingly pursued policies that have contributed to an unstable future climate, a public resource, therefore denying their future constitutional rights. As Ann Carlson, a professor of environmental law at the University of California Los Angeles, told Vox recently: "That's the brilliance of having children as the plaintiffs…they're arguing about the future of the planet." If successful, it will be a landmark case finally granting rights to the citizens of tomorrow.

What do all these initiatives add up to? We are in the midst of an historic political shift. It is clear that a movement for the rights and interests of future generations is beginning to emerge on a global scale, and is set to gain momentum over coming decades as the twin threats of ecological collapse and technological risk loom ever larger. The dream of a benign dictator is not the only option to deal with our long-term crises. Democracy has taken many forms and been reinvented many times, from the direct democracy of the ancient Greeks to the rise of representative democracy in the 18th century. The next democratic revolution—one that empowers future generations and decolonizes the future—may well be on the political horizon.

VIEWPOINT 4

> "While many of the problems inhibiting effective climate action are political, they aren't really about politicians failing to do anything."

Government Failure to Act Isn't the Main Barrier to Climate Action

Nick Bernards

In this viewpoint by Nick Bernards, he argues that while climate action is definitively a political issue, the lack of success in enacting effective climate action is largely not because of politicians, but because powerful companies in the energy and finance sectors have had an outsized influence on climate policy. Politicians have created and attempted to pass climate legislation in previous decades, but have failed to do so because it would cut into the profits of powerful companies. At the moment, attempts to reduce carbon emissions and find green sources of energy are largely in the hands of private companies rather than the government, and since these companies are profit-motivated they are less invested in enabling highly effective climate action. The interests of these powerful companies must be confronted before effective climate action is possible. Nick Bernards is an associate professor of sustainable global development at the University of Warwick.

"Climate Change: Why Government Failure to Act Isn't the Problem," by Nick Bernards, The Conversation, August 19, 2021. https://theconversation.com/climate-change-why-government-failure-to-act-isnt-the-problem-165899. Licensed under CC BY 4.0 International.

Are Today's Political Systems Ill-Equipped to Deal with Climate Change?

As you read, consider the following questions:

1. According to this viewpoint, why did carbon credits largely fail to cut carbon emissions?
2. What effect did Clean Development Mechanism (CDM)-funded carbon trading have on communities?
3. Why has the push to find energy sources with lower carbon emissions resulted in more mineral extraction?

The recent Intergovernmental Panel on Climate Change (IPCC) report underscored the dire state of the climate crisis, concluding that "immediate, rapid and large-scale reductions in greenhouse gas emissions" are needed to limit global warming even to 1.5°C or 2°C.

The report renewed calls for urgent action and an end to "dithering" by politicians. These echo longstanding arguments which bemoan the lack of "political will" to tackle climate change.

The world absolutely needs to reduce or eliminate emissions, and fast. But while many of the problems inhibiting effective climate action are political, they aren't really about politicians failing to do anything. There has actually been plenty of climate action over the last couple of decades. So far, however, it's largely failed.

Climate Action for Whom?

Different kinds of climate action have different costs and benefits for different people. Because of this, choices about what courses of action to pursue are profoundly shaped by relations of power.

We live in a world marked by severe disparities of wealth and power within and between countries, many of which are rooted in longer histories of colonialism and exploitation. These disparities have often allowed powerful companies in sectors like finance and energy to dictate the course of climate action. This has made it very difficult to pursue measures that might threaten their interests, but which would dramatically reduce emissions—like banning fossil fuel exploration.

Instead, we've had a slew of measures to address climate change which rely on making emissions reductions profitable. But the quickest ways to reduce emissions aren't always the most profitable. And what is profitable for some can be harmful for less powerful people and communities.

One example is carbon credits—permits that allow firms and governments to meet emissions targets and offset their pollution by funding projects that reduce emissions elsewhere, mainly in developing countries. The Clean Development Mechanism (CDM) organised by the U.N. was meant to help reduce emissions this way. As agreed in the 1997 Kyoto Protocol, the CDM was supposed to mobilise investment to install renewable energy, retrofit factories and restore habitats.

While a large market developed for carbon offsets, it failed to substantially reduce emissions. A major reason for this was its reliance on profit-seeking private investors. Many of the projects funded through the CDM were probably profitable on their own— the distribution of CDM credits very closely mirrors patterns of private foreign investment in developing countries, with the vast majority funding projects in China and India.

Only a narrow range of possible emissions reduction projects, which either delivered their own revenue or provided cost savings for existing businesses, were financed as a result. But even these efforts were hampered by the push to create secondary markets for carbon credits, in which banks and financial institutions speculated on the price of credits. This was supposed to create more accurate prices, but instead, it made them more volatile, inhibiting new projects, as it became hard to predict how much the carbon credits they generated were worth.

Carbon trading also privileged the interests of private investors over those of communities near CDM-funded projects. Windfarms built in southern Mexico and financed through the CDM, for instance, privatised communal land, displacing indigenous communities.

Not-So-Sustainable Energy

Another major plank of climate action so far has been incentivising the adoption of new technologies with lower emissions. Governments in developed countries have offered subsidies for people to buy electric cars, or increased funding for research and development of clean energy technology.

It is tempting to think public and private investment in renewable energy might allow governments, businesses and civil society to pull together and fight climate change. But there remain significant obstacles. For one, many of the major energy firms investing in wind and solar power, like Shell and British Petroleum, also supply oil and gas. As long as producing fossil fuels remains profitable, these firms will resist efforts to stop selling them.

More importantly, shifting to fully renewable energy sources would require mineral extraction on a truly massive scale to supply the materials for batteries, wiring and other components of solar panels and wind turbines. Recent estimates suggest that meeting current global energy demand with 100% renewable energy would take more cobalt, lithium, and nickel than is known to exist on earth.

A scramble for these minerals is already underway. Demand for batteries in phones, laptops, and electric cars has triggered a rush to establish industrial mines in the southeast of the Democratic Republic of Congo, where the majority of the world's known reserves of cobalt are found.

Foreign-owned industrial mines employ very few Congolese workers and the profits largely accumulate abroad. Some communities have been removed to make way for mining operations. Small-scale mining by local people, often operating without permits or formal mineral rights and using their own tools, has become the main means by which cobalt has benefited local livelihoods.

But according to media and activist reports, child labor is rife in these smaller mines. Meanwhile, the cobalt boom has been linked to landslides, river pollution, and deforestation, and locals have suffered widespread exposure to toxic mining dust in the air and in food and drinking water.

Some firms, including manufacturers of cars and electronics, as well as financial institutions involved in trading cobalt, have tried to minimise the negative effects of mining. Most of these programs focus on tackling child labor, by certifying that cobalt was extracted from industrial mines rather than from the small-scale mines where most of the problem exists. But replacing smaller mines with industrial-scale ones wouldn't necessarily benefit mining communities.

Climate action so far has failed to confront the interests of powerful businesses and governments, while passing costs on to vulnerable people and places which have contributed very little to the climate crisis. If we want results, we may need to go beyond simply demanding action and instead focus on changing the way the global economy is organised and governed.

VIEWPOINT 5

> "The Supreme Court based its decision on the 'major questions doctrine'—a fairly recent judge-made rule that a federal agency needs very explicit direction from Congress before it can take an action of great economic or political significance."

The Supreme Court Creates a New Obstacle for Climate Action

Michael Gerrard

In this viewpoint, Michael Gerrard discusses the Supreme Court's 2021 ruling on West Virginia v. EPA, *a Supreme Court case that determined that the Environmental Protection Agency (EPA) regulation to shift from coal to cleaner energy sources for electricity generation through the 2015 Clean Power Plan (CPP) gave the EPA too much power. The Court argued that under the "major questions doctrine"—which says that federal agencies need explicit directions from Congress before it can take actions of economic significance—the EPA was not specific enough in its regulation of the power grid instead of particular power plants. This creates uncertainty about how much direction is enough and gives companies more openings to challenge government action in court. However, despite the challenges the government faces in enacting environmental regulations as a result of this ruling, Gerrard explains that it still has a number of tools to*

"A New Twist in the US Clean Energy Saga," by Michael Gerrard, Pictet Asset Management, July 2022. Reprinted by permission.

take action. Michael Gerrard is the founder and faculty director of the Sabin Center for Climate Change Law at Columbia University.

As, you read, consider the following questions:

1. What was the 2015 Clean Power Plan?
2. Before 2022, when was the last time Congress enacted a major environmental law?
3. According to Gerrard, what other tools does the U.S. government have to fight climate change?

The legal framework underpinning the U.S.'s environmental policies has a long and complex history.

One of U.S. President Barack Obama's signature efforts to fight climate change was the 2015 Clean Power Plan (CPP), a regulation of the Environmental Protection Agency (EPA) to shift electricity generation away from coal and toward cleaner sources of energy. Donald Trump ran for president on a pledge to repeal the CPP, and once he took office, he was true to his word and replaced it with a much weaker rule.

On January 19, 2021, the day before Joe Biden was inaugurated as U.S. president, the U.S. Court of Appeals for the District of Columbia Circuit threw out the Trump administration's measures, ruling they did not comply with the Clean Air Act's mandate to reduce air pollution. In response, the Biden government said it was not going to reinstate the CPP because it had become largely obsolete, and vowed to come up with a different set of rules to move the U.S. away from coal.

The U.S. environmental community's hopes were dealt an unexpected blow on October 29, 2021, however, when the U.S. Supreme Court announced that it was going to review the Court of Appeals decision, even before EPA issued its new rules. That led to widespread anxiety that the Supreme Court—now with a 6-3 conservative majority, including three Trump appointees—would take away most or all of EPA's powers to fight climate change.

The Supreme Court issued its decision on June 30, 2022, by the expected 6-3 vote. In a case called *West Virginia v. EPA*, the Court ruled against EPA, but not as harshly as had been feared. The Court declared that EPA had gone too far with the CPP, but it left its other authorities largely untouched.

The Supreme Court based its decision on the "major questions doctrine"—a fairly recent judge-made rule that a federal agency needs very explicit direction from Congress before it can take an action of great economic or political significance. A general mandate to solve a big problem is not enough. Though the Supreme Court had ruled in a landmark 2007 decision called *Massachusetts v. EPA* that the Clean Air Act requires the EPA to regulate greenhouse gases, this time the Court said the statute wasn't specific enough to authorize the CPP, because that went beyond regulating specific power plants, one at a time, to governing the entire electric grid as an interconnected system.

A New Obstacle for Clean Energy

Requiring great specificity from Congress is a big problem. Until August 2022, Congress had not enacted a major new environmental law since 1990.

The partisan divide between Democrats (who generally favor strong environmental rules) and Republicans (who generally oppose them) had grown so wide that Congress became paralyzed on this issue, and on many others. To the surprise of almost everyone, in August, Congress passed—and President Biden signed—the Inflation Reduction Act, which provides massive funding for clean energy programs. However, not a single Republican in either chamber voted for this bill, and it consists almost entirely of financial assistance and tax credits; it creates no new regulatory programs, except for one about methane.

Another big problem is that no one really knows what is a "major question" and what isn't. That uncertainty will fuel lawsuits. The U.S. has much more litigation challenging government action than any other country; a database maintained by the Sabin Center for Climate Change Law shows that of the nearly 2,000 lawsuits around the world related to climate change, more than 70 percent are in the U.S.

In the wake of the West Virginia decision, those opposing federal action are likely to raise the major questions doctrine, in addition to their other claims. For example, the Securities and Exchange Commission has proposed an important rule mandating disclosure of companies' direct and indirect greenhouse gas emissions. When that rule is issued in final form, it will surely be challenged in court, and one of the arguments will be that the SEC needs clearer direction from Congress.

This uncertainty will extend beyond environmental and energy rules. Federal actions on food and drugs, health and safety, telecommunications, and other areas will be subject to attack. That is not to say that the lawsuits will succeed, or that the federal rules will be held in abeyance while the litigation proceeds.

But it will be difficult for companies to be confident what rules apply to them.

Despite all of this, the U.S. government still has many tools to fight climate change. The West Virginia decision should not affect the ability to require cleaner and more fuel efficient motor vehicles. It does not impair EPA regulation of greenhouse gas emissions from stationary sources like power plants and factories that also emit other air pollutants. It does not mean that EPA can no longer regulate the other environmental impacts of coal plants and coal mines—air pollution, coal ash, heated water and other types of air pollution.

Government subsidies and incentives for renewable energy, and regulations requiring greater energy efficiency in appliances and industrial equipment, were not touched by the decision, and in August the Inflation Reduction Act added greatly to the subsidies and incentives. State and local governments retain all their powers.

Therefore one tool has been removed from the toolbox of U.S. climate regulation, but many remain. And the movement toward clean energy will continue and accelerate.

Periodical and Internet Sources Bibliography

The following articles have been selected to supplement the diverse views presented in this chapter.

Zack Colman, "New Study Raises the Heat on Exxon's Secret Climate Research," *Politico*, January 12, 2023. https://www.politico.com/news/2023/01/12/exxonmobil-scientists-study-climate-change-global-warming-00077483.

Christiana Figureres, Yvo de Boer, and Michael Zammit Cutajar, "For 50 Years Governments Have Failed to Act on Climate Change. No More Excuses," the *Guardian*, June 2, 2022. https://www.theguardian.com/commentisfree/2022/jun/02/for-50-years-governments-have-failed-to-act-on-climate-change-no-more-excuses.

Samantha Gross, "Barriers to Achieving US Climate Goals Are More Political than Technical," Brookings Institution, May 10, 2021. https://www.brookings.edu/blog/planetpolicy/2021/05/10/barriers-to-achieving-us-climate-goals-are-more-political-than-technical/.

Amy Harder, "Why Climate Change Is So Hard to Tackle: The Global Problem," Axios, August 19, 2019. https://www.axios.com/2019/08/19/why-climate-change-is-so-hard-to-tackle-the-global-problem.

Bella Issacs-Thomas, "We Have the Tools to Save the Planet from Climate Change. Politics Is Getting in the Way, New IPCC Report Says," PBS News, April 4, 2022. https://www.pbs.org/newshour/science/we-have-the-tools-to-save-the-planet-from-climate-change-politics-is-getting-in-the-way-new-ipcc-report-says.

Peter Jackson, "From Stockholm to Kyoto: A Brief History of Climate Change," *UN Chronicle*, June 2007. https://www.un.org/en/chronicle/article/stockholm-kyoto-brief-history-climate-change.

Elaine Kamarck, "The Challenging Politics of Climate Change," Brookings Institution, September 23, 2019. https://www.brookings.edu/research/the-challenging-politics-of-climate-change/.

Jiang Kejun and Valérie Masson-Delmotte, "Climate Change Is a Problem of Politics, Not Science," Euractiv, December 14, 2018. https://www.euractiv.com/section/climate-environment/opinion/climate-change-is-a-problem-of-politics-not-science/.

Ezra Klein, "What If American Democracy Fails the Climate Crisis?" *New York Times*, June 22, 2021. https://www.nytimes.com/2021/06/22/magazine/ezra-klein-climate-crisis.html.

Elizabeth Kolbert, "How Did Fighting Climate Change Become a Partisan Issue?" *New Yorker*, August 22, 2022. https://www.newyorker.com/magazine/2022/08/22/how-did-fighting-climate-change-become-a-partisan-issue.

Shannon Osaka, "Is the US Uniquely Bad at Tackling Climate Change?" Grist, January 6, 2022. https://grist.org/politics/is-american-democracy-uniquely-bad-at-tackling-climate-change/.

Victor Tangermann, "Exxon Scientists Knew about Climate Change for Decades While Company Denied It," Futurism, January 13, 2023. https://futurism.com/exxon-scientists-global-warming-denied.

Justin Worland, "How Climate Change May Be Contributing to Our Political Instability," *Time*, September 15, 2020. https://time.com/5888866/climate-change-wildfires-political-instability/.

CHAPTER 2

Who Should Pay for the Impacts of Climate Change?

Chapter Preface

Climate change has an impact on the entire planet; no place is safe. But the pain is not evenly distributed. Island nations will suffer more from rising sea levels. Areas that are already experiencing droughts or floods will suffer more as extreme weather intensifies. In addition, poor nations and poor communities and individuals in rich nations will suffer more from extreme weather and other effects of climate change. It takes money to prepare for disasters and money to recover from them. Rich nations are rich in part because of their industrial activities, many of which are harmful to the environment. Poor nations contribute a much smaller proportion of global carbon emissions, yet feel the impact more severely.

According to some, all of this makes the issue of climate change into something of a social justice issue. But even if that is given, the solutions aren't at all obvious. Should rich nations pay for the cost of rebuilding in poor nations after disasters? Should rich nations pay for climate mitigation efforts in poor nations? Or would that expose rich nations to legal jeopardy? Do poor nations have the right to have "their turn" developing their economies, even if it means adding to global warming? After all, rich nations had their change to build their economies at the expense of the planet. While these issues may seem straightforward, the details are complex.

In November of 2022, at the 2022 United Nations Climate Change Conference in Egypt, the world's rich nations agreed to establish a fund to help poor countries cope with the ravages of global warming. At the time this volume was published, the details were still being worked out. However, one part of the plan is that in exchange for contributing to the fund, rich nations will not be help legally liable for climate-change related disasters.

The viewpoints in this chapter look at these issues from a variety of perspectives, suggesting different approaches and different potential solutions.

Viewpoint 1

> *"Climate change will negatively and disproportionately impact poor and marginalized people within national borders as well as cause conflicts between nations, regions and cities that are more or less vulnerable to climate disruptions. How should ethics inform these questions?"*

Climate Change Brings Ethical Responsibilities

William S. Lynn

In this viewpoint by William S. Lynn—which was written while the UN Climate Change Conference was taking place in 2015 in Paris, France—the author discusses the ethical questions that have arose about who bears responsibility in fighting climate change and mitigating its effects. Lynn explains that poor and marginalized groups of people are disproportionately affected by the effects of climate change on both a national and international level. Carbon taxes are meant to reduce emissions and raise money to fight climate change, but the questions of whether consumers, corporations, or everyone should bear the cost is a topic of contention. Lynn also brings up the issue of ethical responsibilities to other species and

"The Ethics of Climate Change: What We Owe People—and the Rest of the Planet," by William S. Lynn, The Conversation, December 8, 2015. https://theconversation.com/the-ethics-of-climate-change-what-we-owe-people-and-the-rest-of-the-planet-51785. Licensed under CC BY 4.01 International.

the rest of nature in discussions about climate change. William S. Lynn is a research scientist specializing in animal and sustainability ethics at Clark University.

As you read, consider the following questions:

1. In this viewpoint, how are climate justice and climate equity defined?
2. According to this viewpoint, what is Indian Prime Minister Narendra Modi's perspective on the use of fossil fuels among developing nations?
3. According to Lynn, what is one issue with national commitments to reduce carbon emissions?

Ethics is a particularly relevant if underreported topic of conversation at the United Nations conference on climate change in Paris. While technical disputes grab the lion's share of attention, we should not forget the moral reasons we must address global warming—because of the substantial harm it does and will do to the human and nonhuman world.

Climate justice refers to the disproportional impact of climate change on poor and marginalized populations, while climate equity refers to who should bear the burden of responsibility for addressing climate change.

These twin concerns have both intranational and international dimensions. Climate change will negatively and disproportionately impact poor and marginalized people *within* national borders as well as cause conflicts *between* nations, regions and cities that are more or less vulnerable to climate disruptions.

How should ethics inform these questions?

Fairness and Costs

Any economic discussion regarding lowering greenhouse gas emissions needs to address social justice.

For example, a carbon tax is recognized by economists as the most efficient means for pricing and reducing carbon emissions. As with all taxes, the cost of such a tax would be passed on from businesses to consumers. Who then should bear this cost? Should the tax be borne equally by all, or be paid by the wealthy and corporations who benefit most from dumping carbon into the atmosphere?

Similarly, islands and coastal areas close to sea level face the prospect of catastrophic inundation and storm damage from rising seas and the increasing strength of hurricanes and typhoons. These are communities geographically vulnerable through no fault of their own.

Should they bear the cost of building the infrastructure—sea walls, raised roads, pumping stations—to improve their resilience? Indeed, some island nations must be prepared to evacuate their entire population. Should they alone bear the huge costs and social risks of climate migration?

Who Shoulders the Burden?

With respect to climate equity, a heated debate has arisen over who should take the most responsibility for climate action. Historically, the global north of industrialized nations (the United States and western Europe) has contributed most to global warming.

Some in the global south, including India's Prime Minister Narendra Modi, argue that *increasing* developing countries' use of fossil fuels is necessary to lift millions out of poverty.

Indeed, India's latest negotiating position is to demand that the global north make steep carbon cuts so that India may continue to pollute for economic development. India would reduce the "carbon intensity" of its economic activity, but would not make cuts for decades as its total greenhouse gas pollution grows.

Such a position has led to a great deal of bickering, not only over who should shoulder the economic and social burden, but how sustainable development should move forward.

Moreover, the national commitments to reduce carbon emissions are essentially voluntary and self-policed. Taken together, they do not limit global warming to two degrees Celsius, a threshold we cannot exceed if we hope to maintain a planet of prosperous societies and flourishing biodiversity. Far preferable is to draw down greenhouse gas emissions for a safer 1.5C increase, a position that is not even being discussed.

Inequalities of Wealth and Power

There are a host of other moral issues related to climate justice and equity.

One is that conservative politicians, corporate interests and their think tank sycophants have knowingly peddled climate denial for decades. This is straight-out malfeasance and malpractice in terms of political and research ethics.

It's the 1 Percent Again

The richest 1% of people in the world produce more than double the amount of carbon emissions from the poorest half, according to a new report.

The findings, based on research carried out by the charity Oxfam and the Stockholm Environment Institute, found that the wealthiest people have a significantly greater impact on carbon pollution and climate change compared to the 3.1 billion of the world's poorest people.

The study looked at carbon emissions added to the atmosphere between 1990 and 2015. It found that the richest 10% of people were responsible for a massive 52% (just over half) of worldwide emissions during this period.

The richest 1% were responsible for 15% of emissions, while the poorest half of the world had collectively created just 7% of carbon pollution.

Who Should Pay for the Impacts of Climate Change?

Add to that the rising inequalities of wealth at home and abroad. Global elites will suffer few consequences and have little incentive to act for the good of the public or the planet. This will further exacerbate ethical and political fractures between climate haves and have-nots.

In addition, urban sprawl and ongoing population growth will consume an area the size of Mongolia by the end of the century, with all that entails for environmental degradation and the economic needs of the urban poor.

We will also see the geographical expansion of diseases, food insecurity, social unrest, resource wars, climate refugees and billion-dollar climate disasters, all at a huge cost to human life and suffering. Moral and political fatigue will slowly reduce our capacity to properly care and respond to this growing set of crises.

> Although restrictions introduced as a result of the coronavirus have seen emissions fall, the difference between the levels produced by the richest and poorest in society is still huge.
>
> "The over-consumption of a wealthy minority is fuelling the climate crisis yet it is poor communities and young people who are paying the price," said Tim Gore, Head of Climate Policy at Oxfam and author of the report.
>
> He believes more needs to be done to protect the groups least responsible for the climate crisis, including the poor and vulnerable.
>
> He also says more measures should be introduced by those in charge to cut emissions produced by the rich, including a sales tax on private jets and super yachts.
>
> "Governments must curb the emissions of the wealthy through taxes and bans on luxury carbon such as SUVs and frequent flights. Revenues should be invested in public services and low carbon sectors to create jobs, and help end poverty," he said.
>
> "Climate change: How the richest countries contribute to it," BBC, September 23, 2020.

Obligations to Other Species

Yet, neither climate justice nor equity speaks to the other aspect of climate ethics, namely our moral duties to other animals and the broader community of life.

Global warming is undoubtedly the product of human causes. We not only brought this problem on ourselves, but foisted it onto the natural world with nary a thought for the ethics of doing so.

The dominant rhetoric might decry what global warming will do to human societies, but it rarely speaks of what it does and will do to the creatures and ecosystems with whom we share the earth. Pope Francis' Ladauto Si is a sterling exception in this regard. The intrinsic value of people, animals and nature means that we have a direct duty to the nonhuman world to address climate change as a matter of moral urgency.

Interspecies responsibilities also put questions of climate justice and equity into a larger moral landscape, changing how we see our common and differentiated responsibilities to combat climate change.

Fights over climate justice and equity are essentially about what we owe each other as human beings. The rich, Western, industrialized countries should share the largest burden not only for historical reasons, but because they are wealthy enough to absorb the costs for the long-term well-being of themselves and the global south.

But arguing over what nation or social group should be held culpable can distract from the urgent need to act for the well-being of people and the planet now.

The Rest of Nature

Emergent industrialized economies like India's also have a rapidly increasing responsibility to cut their own global emissions of greenhouse gases. Island nations have made this point eloquently in the face of bickering between the global north and south.

And India's current negotiating position seems more focused on better positioning the economy for the global stage, than it is in meeting its common if differentiated responsibilities. India is not alone in this. Its elites are simply outspoken in their anthropocentric self-interest.

The same critique applies to how we ought to care for other animals and the rest of nature. Their fate should not be hostage to a narrowing argument about culpability. It is rather a matter of responding morally to the needs of others—human or nonhuman—in the face of climate crisis. What matters most is not apportioning blame and seeking advantage, but making things right.

Global warming threatens the well-being of people and the planet, raising crucial issues of ethics and public policy that we ignore at our peril. Left unchecked, or by doing too little too late, climate change will haunt future generations and leave a despoiled earth as our legacy.

VIEWPOINT 2

> "Most importantly, rich nations have an ethical responsibility to fix the crisis they caused."

Rich, Polluting Countries Owe the Developing World

Courtney Lindwall

In this viewpoint, Courtney Lindwall explains the pledge wealthy nations made at the 2009 UN climate summit in Copenhagen, Denmark. At this conference, rich nations promised to mobilize $100 billion per year starting in 2020 to help developing countries meet the demands of addressing the impacts of climate change. These countries failed to keep their promise by not meeting their funding target and by not defining what they would pay for or how to measure success. In reality, developing countries need much more money than this to adapt to climate change, but $100 billion annually would be an important first step. By not meeting the $100 billion goal, rich countries breach global trust and fail to meet their ethical responsibility. Courtney Lindwall is a writer and editor at the Natural Resources Defense Council.

As you read, consider the following questions:

1. According to this viewpoint, how many rich nations are responsible for half of all historical CO_2 emissions?

"Rich, Polluting Nations Still Owe the Developing World," by Courtney Lindwall, Natural Resources Defense Council, January 21, 2022. Reprinted by permission.

2. How did countries agree on the $100 billion target, according to this viewpoint?
3. How much money do developing countries actually need for climate adaptation, according to this viewpoint?

There's no denying it: Wealthy countries, particularly the United States and Western European nations, have emitted the lion's share of greenhouse gases that led to the climate crisis. In fact, just 23 developed countries are responsible for half of all historical CO_2 emissions. Yet it's developing nations that are being hit hardest by the effects—and are the least ready to respond.

This is why rich nations made a promise at the 2009 United Nations climate summit, or COP15, in Copenhagen. Together, they agreed to mobilize $100 billion per year, officially beginning in 2020, to help developing countries reduce their emissions and adapt to the impacts of climate change.

Then they broke their promise.

They not only failed to meet the 2020 funding target but also did not clearly define what they would pay for or how to measure success. Here's what you need to know about this funding pledge and why, even with all its flaws, climate experts believe it remains critical.

Q: Why $100 billion?

A: As part of the 2009 Copenhagen climate accord, experts tried to calculate what it could cost those 23 wealthy countries to fund climate mitigation and adaptation in the developing world. Some deemed the price tag to be as high as $400 billion per year. The agreed-upon $100 billion was "more or less a compromise," says NRDC climate strategist Brendan Guy, who was part of an NRDC team that led a discussion on taking climate finance from pledge to project at the most recent climate conference in Glasgow, COP26.

Yet it remains significant largely because of the political promise it represents.

Q: So how close are countries to hitting this yearly goal?

A: Beginning in 2013, donor countries attempted to ratchet up contributions each year, with the hope of reaching $100 billion by the 2020 start date. But by 2019, they had only mobilized about $80 billion in public and private climate funding, according to the Organization for Economic Cooperation and Development (OECD), an intergovernmental body made up of many of the donor countries. While the data isn't in yet for 2020, some reports predicted that funders would scale back their commitments due to the pandemic.

Even so, these totals paint an incomplete picture, in part because countries have yet to agree on how to divvy up the pie so that all parties pay their fair share. A few organizations have come up with estimates, but the countries themselves haven't endorsed those percentages. There are also competing perspectives for what kind of funding counts toward the goal of $100 billion per year. Some argue that this means the OECD totals are potentially inflated because, in addition to grants, they also include loans, which must be repaid with interest. A few countries that appear to have surpassed their share of funding, like Japan and France, have provided the majority of the money as loans. This is why Oxfam, an international nonprofit focused on alleviating poverty, estimates the total climate funding from 2017–18 is just a third of the OECD's estimates—somewhere between $19 billion to $22.5 billion.

Q: What does the money that is available pay for?

A: The money is supposed to fund both mitigation and adaptation in developing countries, which reduce emissions and help residents cope with expected climate impacts. But even this gets murky—and not just because no single organization tracks the projects that are funded. The other problem is that countries define mitigation and adaptation differently. Yes, money that goes toward the installation of solar panels or the erection of seawalls feels clear cut. But what about the building of new roads, which have been labeled by some countries as "climate-relevant," or, as was included in Japan's tally in 2017, funding for "cleaner" coal plants in Bangladesh? This is why Oxfam estimates that true climate-related finance has been significantly overreported.

The balance between adaptation and mitigation is also fraught. Adaptation is notoriously harder to fund, particularly from private sources—likely because those projects tend to mostly benefit local residents and don't generate significant profits. In 2019, for example, just 25 percent of climate finance went toward adaptation.

Whether these projects are ultimately successful at achieving their goals is another data problem. Not only is success project-specific—ranging from, say, emissions reductions to the prevention of climate gentrification—but also data on outcomes remains challenging to collect and often lags years behind.

Q: Did last year's COP26 in Glasgow help address any of the current obstacles?

A: The $100 billion broken promise certainly loomed large, and some countries took the opportunity to up their commitments. For example, ahead of Glasgow, President Joe Biden proposed $11.4 billion in annual U.S. climate funding by 2024, but that requires congressional approval, which remains far from a sure thing. It's also still only a portion of what is actually owed: The United States has emitted a quarter of all historical emissions, according to estimates from the World Resources Institute, and should pay as much as 47 percent of that $100 billion per year.

At COP26, developing countries also demanded additional money for "loss and damage"—the costs accrued from climate impacts beyond what could be adapted to—but no specific funding promise was made. (There were some inroads, thankfully, on increasing the share of adaptation finance.) Countries also attempted to remedy some of the data dilemmas with new transparency and tracking requirements but again failed to nail down uniform definitions on what counts as climate finance. At best, wealthy nations suggested that the $100 billion target would likely be met by 2023 and that funding should increase from there.

Q: How much do developing nations truly need for climate adaptation?

A: The $100 billion per year was always a starting point that would increase over time. And that's good because the U.N.'s Intergovernmental Panel on Climate Change (IPCC) estimates that developing nations will need as much as $300 billion per year just for adaptation by decade's end. The IPCC's estimates for the world economy to transition to clean energy at the pace required to keep warming within the 1.5 degree Celsius threshold put the cost at up to $3.8 trillion annually by 2050. And that's still trillions less than a worst-case climate scenario.

Q: So why does the $100 billion remain so important?

A: NRDC's Guy calls the $100 billion a pragmatic, political, and ethical imperative. The whole world needs to transition away from fossil fuels—and fast, if we're to keep warming below 1.5 degrees Celsius. But developing countries don't always have the resources to do so, or doing so may require them to trade off short-term economic gains that could be made through keeping older, polluting infrastructure in play. The money is a pragmatic necessity to reduce emissions quickly enough and protect people in the process.

Politically, not meeting the $100 billion goal represents a significant breach of global trust when climate action requires steadfast international cooperation.

Most importantly, rich nations have an ethical responsibility to fix the crisis they caused. "There is a clear and compelling moral case to help countries most at risk, such as small islands and countries that have contributed virtually nothing to the problem in terms of emissions," Guy says. Investing $100 billion per year represents the bare minimum toward righting such a catastrophic wrong.

VIEWPOINT 3

> "Industrialized countries have been reluctant to commit funding, concerned it could lead to being legally liable for the impacts of climate change. At this year's climate talks, developing countries say it's a crucial part of climate justice."

Wealthy Nations Are Reluctant to Financially Commit to Helping Developing Nations Affected by Climate Change

Lauren Sommer

In this viewpoint, Lauren Sommer explains the argument developing countries are making for why rich countries should compensate them for the effects of climate change. This would involve contributing to a loss and damage fund for the extreme weather events developing countries disproportionately face. Even though a loss and damage fund was discussed at the 2015 Paris climate talks, rich nations have been largely reluctant to create one out of fear of being held financially and legally liable for all effects of climate change. But developing nations argue that this financial aid is essential for them to recover from disasters caused by climate change and owed to them because of the West's responsibility for causing climate change. Lauren Sommer is a correspondent for NPR's Science Desk.

©2021 National Public Radio, Inc. NPR news report titled "Developing nations say they›re owed for climate damage. Richer nations aren›t budging" by Lauren Sommer was originally published on NPR.org on November 11, 2021, and is used with the permission of NPR. Any unauthorized duplication is strictly prohibited.

Who Should Pay for the Impacts of Climate Change?

As you read, consider the following questions:

1. What would a loss and damage fund help pay for?
2. According to this viewpoint, what is the issue with the $100 billion wealthy countries have pledged to pay developing countries each year?
3. What recent scientific development has played a role in loss and damage conversations?

Barbados Prime Minister Mia Mottley wants richer countries to stop throwing garbage in her yard and then telling her to clean it up.

The garbage, in this case, is greenhouse gas emissions that fuel more extreme storms and hurricanes, causing widespread destruction which can cost billions of dollars. At the Glasgow climate negotiations, Mottley is leading a push for richer countries to compensate poorer ones for the "loss and damage" caused by climate change.

Their argument is this: developed countries, like the U.S. and those in the European Union, are responsible for most of the heat-trapping emissions pumped into the atmosphere since the Industrial Revolution. Developing countries have lower emissions, but are still bearing the brunt of a hotter climate through more severe heat waves, floods and droughts.

"It is unjust and it is immoral," Mottley said at the summit. "It is wrong."

To help compensate for that, developing countries are asking richer ones to contribute to a loss and damage fund. The money could offer payment for things that are irrevocably lost, like lives or the extinction of species. It could also help countries with the cost of rebuilding after storms, replacing damaged crops, or relocating entire communities at risk.

While loss and damage was discussed at the Paris climate talks in 2015, progress has been slow. Industrialized countries have been reluctant to commit funding, concerned it could lead to being legally liable for the impacts of climate change. At this year's climate talks, developing countries say it's a crucial part of climate justice.

"Providing finance for loss and damage is the very least that wealthy countries can and should do," says Raeed Ali, a climate activist from Fiji and part of the Loss and Damage Youth Coalition. "But to do this, they will have to acknowledge that they are responsible for this. And I think that is something they are not willing to do."

Few Resources to Recover from Disasters

For countries where much of the population lives in poverty, extreme weather can be a devastating blow. Individuals have little savings to rebuild, while governments with few resources struggle to secure the millions of dollars needed to help communities recover.

"In Fiji, we are at the forefront of the climate crisis," Ali says. "So every single person knows about climate change because it's a daily reality for us."

Ali says while his grandparents only remember experiencing one category 5 cyclone in their lives, he's already seen three. And with rising sea levels threatening to make villages uninhabitable, a handful in Fiji have already been relocated, and more than 40 are slated to be moved, he said.

Some countries are being hit by back-to-back disasters. In 2015, the Caribbean island nation of Dominica was hit by tropical storm Erika, causing more than $400 million in damage, equal to 90% of the country's gross domestic product. Two years later, Hurricane Maria slammed the island, damaging 90% of the country's housing stock.

In the Gambia in West Africa, where the majority of people in rural areas depend on agriculture, crop failures can be catastrophic. Because the country's main river flows into the ocean, rising sea levels are pushing saltwater farther and farther upriver, making it harder to get freshwater.

"It's really affecting the farming communities," says Isatou Camara, a climate negotiator for the Gambia in West Africa.

"Because of sea level rise, we have saltwater intruding into our river which is affecting farm production, especially rice farming which is usually done along the riverside."

This is what the world looks like if we pass the crucial 1.5-degree climate threshold

Developed countries have promised $100 billion per year in "climate finance" to help poorer nations reduce their emissions through things like renewable energy and sustainable agriculture. They've yet to fully deliver on that goal, since each country determines its own contribution.

But many developing countries say that funding doesn't help with the climate impacts they're already experiencing, which is why a separate loss and damage fund is needed. In 2020, natural disasters caused $210 billion in damage worldwide.

Assigning Liability for Climate Change

At the 2015 Paris climate summit, countries signed an agreement recognizing the need to address loss and damage. But developed countries pushed to include language that specified it did not "provide a basis for any liability." They feared that admitting responsibility for their share of heat-trapping pollution would expose them to paying developing nations every time a disaster hit.

"It's always something developed countries have been very cautious about exactly because they don't want it to be a precedent for international courts," Maria Antonia Tigre, a fellow at Columbia University's Sabin Center for Climate Change Law. "They really do want to avoid that responsibility because it can be endless."

Recent advances in climate change science have upped the pressure. While many climate studies examine long-term trends, researchers at the World Weather Attribution initiative study whether climate change has amplified an extreme weather event in the weeks or months after it hits.

Hurricane Harvey, which released a deluge of rain on Houston in 2017, was made 15% more intense by climate change, they found. This past summer, the severe heat wave in the Pacific Northwest that caused dozens of deaths was virtually impossible without the added boost of human-caused greenhouse gas emissions.

"The fact that we are able to pinpoint the climate fingerprint in specific things that hurt us today, I think, is a very important element in the current loss and damage conversation," says Maarten van Aalst, director of the Red Cross Red Crescent Climate Center and a scientist with the World Weather Attribution initiative. "It has changed the conversation over the past years."

Van Aalst is quick to point out that assigning blame is a complex question. While a storm's destruction is caused by its strength, it also occurs if the buildings and homes aren't built to handle storms. Some communities aren't designed to endure the kinds of events that occurred even before the effects of climate change started to be felt.

Still, court cases are underway around the world to establish liability for climate change, either seeking damages from governments or fossil fuel companies.

"The uncertainty of science was one of the main arguments that was always used by states to avoid responsibility," says Tigre. "And that's a bridge that's now crossed."

No Show of Funding for Loss and Damage

At the Glasgow summit, Scotland announced a major milestone for addressing loss and damage needs. It offered 2 million pounds in funding, the first-of-its-kind.

"That is in the right direction," said Sonam Wangdi of Bhutan, who chairs a group of the 46 poorer countries at the talks. "It's going to be very clear that there should be separate funds for loss and damage, and it should not be mixed with all the other funds."

Still, other funding commitments haven't followed yet. While the U.S. has formally recognized the need to address loss and damage, a senior U.S. official says the country doesn't support creating a dedicated new fund.

Instead of waiting for voluntary offers, Barbados Prime Minister Mottley is proposing using 1% tax on sales revenues from fossil fuels, which she estimates could raise $70 billion per year. Some are simply hoping that countries invest in the United Nation's Santiago Network, which was set up in 2019 to handle loss and damage issues. But without enough staffing and funding, it exists mainly symbolically today.

Even if developed countries offer new support for a loss and damage fund, they could still be held liable for the impacts of climate change. At a press conference in Glasgow, the island nations of Tuvalu and Antigua and Barbuda announced they're forming a new commission to enable small island countries to seek compensation through international courts.

Viewpoint 4

> "I believe that by paying closer attention to the strengths and weaknesses of climate finance delivery channels and matching them to countries' needs, the international community can make a real difference in the fight against climate change."

Rich Countries Need to Get Serious and Specific About Climate Finance

Rishikesh Ram Bhandary

In this viewpoint, Rishikesh Ram Bhandary considers the findings of the 2022 Intergovernmental Panel on Climate Change (IPCC) report and what it says about the damage caused by climate change. Unsurprisingly, it found that developing countries are continuing to suffer a greater share of the effects from climate change. This makes the issue of climate finance and how to direct money to these countries even more urgent. The author considers the major channels of climate finance and looks at the pros and cons of each. Ultimately, more effort needs to be put into defining what climate finance is, raising the available funds, and researching the impacts of climate finance. Rishikesh Ram Bhandary is

"Wealthy countries still haven't met their $100 billion pledge to help poor countries face climate change, and the risks are rising", by Rishikesh Ram Bhandary, The Conversation, February 28, 2022. https://theconversation.com/wealthy-countries-still-havent-met-their-100-billion-pledge-to-help-poor-countries-face-climate-change-and-the-risks-are-rising-173229#:~:text=After%20another%20year%20of%20record-breaking%20temperatures%20and%20extreme,to%20help%20poorer%20countries%20deal%20with%20climate%20change. Licensed under CC BY 4.0 International.

Who Should Pay for the Impacts of Climate Change?

Assistant Director of the Global Economic Governance Initiative of the Global Development Policy Center at Boston University.

As you read, consider the following questions:

1. According to this viewpoint, how much money in climate finance went to developing countries in 2019?
2. According to this viewpoint, what are the three major channels for climate finance?
3. What are the three ways the author suggests moving the climate finance conversation forward?

After another year of record-breaking temperatures and extreme weather disasters, wealthy countries are under pressure to make good on their commitment to mobilize US$100 billion a year to help poorer countries deal with climate change.

Developed countries now project that they won't meet that pledge until 2023 – three years late and still woefully short of the real need.

A new report from the Intergovernmental Panel on Climate Change, released Feb. 28, 2022, provides more evidence of what billions of people are facing: Developing countries that have contributed the least to climate change are suffering the most from it, and the damage is escalating.

Small island states and low-lying coastal areas are losing land to rising seas. Flooding from extreme storms is wiping out people's livelihoods in Africa and Asia. Heat waves are harming people who have no access to cooling, killing crops and affecting marine life communities rely on. Documents from the United Nations suggest that the cost for low-income countries to adapt to these and other climate impacts far exceeds the promised $100 billion a year.

What's less clear is how much impact the climate finance already flowing to these countries, estimated at $79.6 billion in 2019, is having. There is an overwhelming lack of data, as well as evidence that countries have been supporting projects that could harm the climate with money they count as "climate finance."

Part of the problem is how that money gets from donors to projects in countries in need. I have worked closely with developing countries seeking help to deal with climate change. I believe that by paying closer attention to the strengths and weaknesses of climate finance delivery channels and matching them to countries' needs, the international community can make a real difference in the fight against climate change.

How Does Climate Finance Flow?

Donor countries have three major channels through which they can route climate finance: bilateral agreements between small groups of countries, international funds like the Green Climate Fund and development banks like the World Bank. Each has benefits and drawbacks.

Bilateral Agreements

First, countries can directly negotiate financing commitments, also known as bilateral agreements. These arrangements allow donors to target specific areas of need and are often more efficient than multilateral agreements, since they involve fewer entities.

For example, at the Glasgow climate conference in November 2021, South Africa and a group of donor countries announced an $8.5 billion effort to help South Africa transition away from coal while increasing renewable energy generation. This deal allowed four national governments and the European Union to come together and craft a package around what South Africa wanted.

Groups of donors have also come together to support national-level financing, though new research suggests these arrangements are underused.

A major drawback of bilateral arrangements is that they can be sensitive to the ebbs and flows of political attention. While issues in the news can attract funding, some countries struggle to get help.

Climate Funds

It is precisely to ensure that countries have regular and consistent access to climate finance that a second option exists: international climate funds.

For example, the U.N.-backed Green Climate Fund is one of the largest and offers universal eligibility. The GCF's scope is also deliberately broad to allow room for programming based on what countries actually need, rather than what is politically attractive at any given moment.

However, the GCF has received pledges totaling only about $18 billion. Developed countries are more likely to route contributions through their own bilateral channels or major development banks than through climate-focused funds.

Development Banks

Finally, major development banks manage significant amounts of climate financing, though there are two key barriers to fully using them.

First, many of these banks have not ambitiously incorporated climate change into their programming. In fact, some came under scrutiny when their joint statement at the Glasgow climate conference did not include specific targets and timetables for ending financing for fossil fuel projects.

Second, most development banks have not been able to effectively mobilize finance from the private sector, in part because of their business models. Development banks tend to prefer projects with lower risk and like to operate in settings where the cost of doing business is not very high. Private-sector funding is crucial to filling the climate finance gap, which means that development banks also need to use instruments that are better able to mobilize private capital such as equity instead of relying too heavily on lending.

Ultimately, splitting climate finance across these different channels is helping to render financing largely ineffective, with developing countries receiving a fraction of the resources necessary to make an impact. Spreading finance thinly across delivery channels means the international community is neither learning from experimentation nor betting on bold ideas.

Getting Serious About Impact

Currently, the efforts to track the $100 billion are focused on counting how much money has actually flowed and where, not what impact has been achieved. Two key issues are complicating efforts to measure the impact.

First, there is no agreed-upon definition of what climate finance is, and countries use their own definitions. For example, in the past Japan counted money for new coal plants that are more efficient than old ones, but still highly polluting, as "climate finance."

Second, some projects focus on helping countries put in place plans and policies. For example, countries have been receiving support to create national adaptation plans. The impact of these planning efforts really relies on how well the plans are implemented.

If the global community is serious about rising to the climate challenge, I believe the conversation needs to move forward in three ways:

1) The scale of financing should far surpass $100 billion.
2) The international community should be more targeted about which sources and channels best meet specific needs.
3) More research is needed to assess the impact of international climate finance so far and establish a sound understanding of which delivery channels work best for which purposes.

The $100 billion in promised funding is much-needed glue that helps hold the U.N. climate process together—it reflects the responsibility borne by countries that have been emitting greenhouse gases for years for driving climate change and the harm to countries that emit little.

VIEWPOINT 5

> "As illustrated by flooded homes and destroyed roofs everywhere from Barbuda to Houston, it is more useful to think of rich and poor (or safe and vulnerable) people rather than countries."

The Focus of Climate Finance and Justice Needs to Shift from Countries to Individuals

John Vogler and Marit Hammond

In this viewpoint, John Vogler and Marit Hammond point out how conversations about climate finance and climate justice tend to focus on countries—rich countries and poor countries. However, which people are affected by climate change and the extreme weather events it causes is not dictated by national borders. Additionally, countries try to protect their own interests rather than focusing on the global community, which creates barriers to effective conversations on climate justice and finance. According to the authors, the focus should shift from discussions about which countries are most impacted by climate change to which individuals suffer the most from its effects, and direct money to poverty reduction around the world to help address this. John Vogler is a professor of international relations at Keele University, where Marit Hammond is a lecturer in environmental politics.

"Who should pay for damage associated with climate change – and who should be compensated?" by John Vogler and Marit Hammond, The Conversation, September 18, 2017. https://theconversation.com/who-should-pay-for-damage-associated-with-climate-change-and-who-should-be-compensated-84028. Licensed under CC BY 4.0 International.

As you read, consider the following questions:

1. According to this viewpoint, where does international debate on climate justice generally occur?
2. According to the authors, what is standing in the way of having effective conversations about climate justice and finance?
3. What do the authors mean by a "cosmopolitan" approach to climate justice?

Hurricanes in the Caribbean and deadly floods across South Asia have once again raised the issue of climate justice.

The association between such events and climate change is now beyond serious question: we have had 30 years of well-founded scientific warnings about the relationship between increasing global temperatures and the incidence and severity of extreme weather. Much more problematic is the question of responsibility for climate change itself, and who should justly pay compensation for the resulting damage.

This is complicated, and there are no clear categories of winners and losers, or responsible and blameless. Consider how the benefits from greenhouse gas emissions are usually divorced from the impacts of climate change, yet hurricane-hit Texas owes much of its wealth to oil. Or look at the extraordinary inequalities among those affected by the storms—most are relatively poor, but a few are among the world's richest people.

The Long Struggle for 'Climate Justice'

International debate on climate justice has usually occurred within the UN, via its Framework Convention on Climate Change (UNFCCC), in a process which led to the Paris Agreement. For much of the time since its inception in 1992 there was a heavy focus on cutting emissions rather than on adaptation to the damaging consequences of climate change.

Responsibility for global warming was usually framed as an obligation for developed states to make the initial moves to reduce their emissions, under the concept of "common but differentiated responsibilities and respective capabilities." Climate justice was seen as something developed states owed less developed states, and were obliged to deliver so the latter had an incentive to cut their emissions, too.

However, by the Bali conference in 2007 it was clear that climate-related sea level rise and extreme weather events were already happening. Adaptation was therefore moved up the agenda alongside emissions cuts. In crude terms, if the developed world wanted a new comprehensive agreement on tackling climate change it would have to provide sufficient guarantees of assistance for the less developed majority. These included a proposed US$100 billion per annum Green Climate Fund but also new form of compensation for "loss and damage for countries vulnerable" to hurricanes and other climate-related disasters.

The "loss and damage" mechanism made it into the 2015 Paris Agreement but has not yet been fully implemented. It was a controversial topic, however, as it raised the question of liability or even reparation for climate damage. Direct responsibility was both difficult to establish and resolutely rejected by developed countries.

Focus on Vulnerable Individuals

The problem is these issues are discussed within the context of a system of self-interested nation states. Climate change requires a global, concerted effort, yet entrenched political structures within each country reinforce competitive and antagonistic outlooks. It is always difficult, for example, to make the case for foreign governmental assistance when this is ranged against domestic poverty.

To be sure, some of the more progressive rich countries do reflect a "communitarian" approach which recognises some moral obligations to assist vulnerable states. This goes beyond the strict minimum in international law of the avoidance of harm, but it certainly does not admit any direct responsibility or liability. At most, this conception of international climate justice is based upon a recognition that the populations of other countries should not be allowed to deteriorate below minimal standards of human existence and is common to other areas of humanitarian assistance and disaster relief.

Yet such state-based thinking remains unable to handle the complexity and all-encompassing nature of climate change. What's needed is an alternative "cosmopolitan" approach to climate justice. Under cosmopolitanism the focus is on individual human beings and their needs and rights, all of whom would exist in one community where nationality is considered irrelevant to moral worth. This means a Bangladeshi farmer or Caribbean fisherman have as much right to be protected from the impact of global warming as someone in Texas or London and, in this sense, cosmopolitan climate justice mirrors the evolution of international human rights principles.

Nationality is often used to indicate development, or vulnerability to natural hazards, yet such categories are essentially misleading. As illustrated by flooded homes and destroyed roofs everywhere from Barbuda to Houston, it is more useful to think of rich and poor (or safe and vulnerable) people rather than countries.

True climate justice will have to reorientate the debate away from state sovereignty and international standing towards a focus on personal harm. A system of individual carbon accounting would also help so that people make a contribution to poverty reduction and disaster relief appropriate to their wealth and lifestyle.

As hurricanes engulf numerous countries at once, and indirectly affect even more, climate change powerfully illustrates the need for creative thinking about a truly global cosmopolitanism in which the avoidance of human suffering comes before self-interest and it is recognised that there are many poor and vulnerable people in "rich countries" and fabulously rich people in "poor countries."

VIEWPOINT 6

> *"Having conducted extensive research about how climate policies are working around the world over the past decade, I believe that the effort to enact a carbon tax is worth it."*

Carbon Taxes Can Work

Gilbert E. Metcalf

In this viewpoint, Gilbert E. Metcalf argues that even though there have been many struggles to impose a carbon tax in the United States—so far without success—it is possible and worthwhile to enact one. A carbon tax makes fossil fuels—which are largely responsible for carbon emissions—more expensive and discourages industries and consumers from using them. In 2016 and 2018 Washington state unsuccessfully tried to become the first U.S. state with a carbon tax. In order to effectively create a carbon tax, Metcalf asserts that lawmakers need to keep fairness in mind, meaning that lower-income households should not have to bear the brunt of carbon taxes. Furthermore, creating a carbon tax and encouraging the move to cleaner energy can actually help create more jobs. Gilbert E. Metcalf is the John DiBiaggio Professor of Citizenship and Public Service and a professor of economics at Tufts University.

"With the Right Guiding Principles, Carbon Taxes Can Work," The Conversation, January 10, 2019. https://theconversation.com/with-the-right-guiding-principles-carbon-taxes-can-work-109328. Licensed under CC BY 4.0 International.

The Politics of Climate

As you read, consider the following questions:

1. According to this viewpoint, what caused the carbon tax ballot initiatives in Washington state to fail in 2016 and 2018?
2. According to Metcalf, what effects have carbon taxes implemented in Sweden and British Columbia, Canada, had on their economies?
3. What example does Metcalf provide of a politician providing guiding framework for policy?

Like most economists, I favor taxing carbon dioxide to cut carbon pollution.

A carbon tax makes fossil fuels like oil and coal more expensive. That, in turn, leads consumers and industries to use less of them. At the same time, it boosts demand for alternative energy sources like wind and solar powered electricity.

With the anti-regulatory Trump administration in power and a Republican majority controlling the Senate, however, no such national policy is imminent. Prospects for statewide efforts may look bleak too, after ballot initiatives in Washington state that would have created the nation's first carbon tax failed in 2016 and 2018.

But other states may move in this direction. Having conducted extensive research about how climate policies are working around the world over the past decade, I believe that the effort to enact a carbon tax is worth it.

The Headwinds

Based on my experience serving as the deputy assistant secretary for environment and energy at the U.S. Treasury Department for two years during the Obama administration, I recognize it won't be easy to enact tough climate policies. Recent events in France underscore this fact. There, President Emmanuel Macron has backed down on the taxes on gasoline, diesel and heating oil that led to waves of so-called yellow vest protests that rocked France and left six protesters dead by mid-December.

Fairness is central to the French protests, which sprang from objections to what came across to many voters as an elitist, out-of-touch central government that has lowered taxes on the rich while hiking taxes on the poor. The 2018 French budget, enacted last December, cut corporate tax rates and wealth taxes while increasing a social levy on all income similar to our payroll taxes. This change skewed taxes away from the rich and made the poor pay more.

This law had already stirred discontent. The hike in fuel taxes, part of a carbon tax initially enacted in 2014, poured fuel on those flames. Framing the increase as an environmental tax did nothing to assuage rural and low-income voters. "We're not anti-environmental," a movement organizer said. "This is a movement against abusive taxation, period."

Meanwhile, the failure of the Washington state ballot initiative illustrates the risks of trying to enact controversial policies at the ballot box. When vast amounts of money poured into the state from big oil corporations like BP to finance a campaign against a carbon tax, thoughtful policy debate was forced to compete with a slick media campaign. Supporters also had to overcome the legacy of a previous failed referendum that pitted climate policy advocates against each other.

The Benefits

Designed correctly, a carbon tax can do more than reduce carbon pollution. It can also make tax codes more fair. Research by a group of economists demonstrates that carbon taxes can be progressive—meaning higher income households pay more in tax per dollar of income than lower-income households.

A carbon tax can also create jobs. Although instituting one in the U.S. would surely speed up the disappearance of U.S. coal mining jobs, that shift would continue no matter what while also expediting the creation of new employment opportunities.

As of today, there are more than twice as many jobs in solar technology than in coal mining.

Finally, taxing carbon is unlikely to hurt the economy. Despite a roughly $135-per-ton tax on carbon dioxide, Sweden is doing just fine. Its GDP has grown by nearly 80 percent since it enacted a carbon tax in the early 1990s, while its emissions have fallen by one-quarter.

Sweden's growth rate has actually exceeded that of the U.S. since 2000 despite high taxes on carbon pollution, in part because Sweden uses the revenue to cut other taxes. And the World Economic Forum finds the two economies to be about equally competitive.

Likewise, British Columbia's carbon tax has not hurt its economy since going into effect in 2008. My analysis indicates, if anything, the tax has boosted growth in the Canadian province. That's because some of the revenue raised was used to cut marginal income tax rates on individuals and the tax bills for small businesses. Another economist based at the University of Calgary found that local employment increased by a small but statistically significant amount.

Politically Feasible

When and if Congress is finally ready to enact a carbon tax in the U.S., it should consider a guiding framework as it debates the elements of the new tax.

President Ronald Reagan understood the power of establishing frameworks to guide tax policy. In his 1984 State of the Union address, he called for a tax reform that would raise no additional revenue but "make the tax base broader, so personal tax rates could come down, not go up."

With that directive, Reagan launched the most significant tax reform in the history of the tax code. His directive made clear that he wanted lower tax rates without sacrificing revenue. This simple framework imposed an important discipline that kept lawmakers on track.

In my new book, "Paying for Pollution: Why a Carbon Tax Is Good for America," I lay out similar guiding principles. In my view, carbon taxation should be revenue-neutral, make the tax code fairer, streamline climate policy and lead to significant emission reductions.

Republicans and Democrats have argued for years over the size of the federal government. It is a debate that should not ensnare climate policy. Revenue neutrality in this context means that all the money raised through a carbon tax should be returned to Americans through some combination of tax cuts and direct payments.

Fairness means that low to moderate income households are not made worse off by the tax. There are many ways to do this including a proposal from the Climate Leadership Council, a policy initiative backed by big corporations like ExxonMobil and General Motors as well as three big environmental groups and former Republican secretaries of State James Baker III and George Shultz, to give all U.S. households the money raised from carbon taxation through carbon dividends.

The government should also provide transitional relief to carbon-intensive industries and regions. The federal government should partner with state and local governments to develop transition plans for these communities.

National climate policies generally include various tax breaks for renewable energy as well as mandates—which in the U.S. primarily consist of state-level renewable portfolio standards. With a carbon tax, it is possible to eliminate some of these overlapping policies and guarantee that emissions decline at the same time.

Reducing greenhouse gas emissions is the whole point of climate policies and therefore the highest priority when implementing them. As the latest U.N. climate report makes clear, cutting carbon pollution everywhere and quickly is an urgent priority. And the Swedish track record suggests that pricing carbon dioxide can help make it happen without hindering economic growth.

VIEWPOINT 7

> "There is an opportunity with this opinion to cement emerging links between climate harms and human rights, which could open up new avenues for litigation either domestically or internationally."

The International Court of Justice Could Advise on What Countries Owe for Their Roles in Climate Change

Jacqueline Peel and Zoe Nay

In this viewpoint, Jacqueline Peel and Zoe Nay consider the United Nation (UN) General Assembly's March 2023 resolution to seek an advisory opinion from the International Court of Justice (ICJ) on a country's climate obligations. The ICJ issues advisory opinions that are not legally binding, but act as general advice on international law. Since the ICJ will look at what a country's climate obligations are and the legal consequences for countries that cause significant climate harm affecting other countries, its advisory opinion could establish firm guidelines about the obligations of countries and encourage countries to reassess their climate goals. Jacqueline Peel is Director of Melbourne Climate Futures at the University of Melbourne in

---

"The UN Is Asking the International Court of Justice for Its Opinion on States' Climate Obligations. What Does This Mean?" by Jacqueline Peel and Zoe Nay, The Conversation, April 3, 2023. https://theconversation.com/the-un-is-asking-the-international-court-of-justice-for-its-opinion-on-states-climate-obligations-what-does-this-mean-202943. Licensed under CC BY 4.0 International.

Australia, where Zoe Nay was a PhD candidate in human rights at the time this viewpoint was published.

As you read, consider the following questions:

1. How many members of the UN General Assembly supported the resolution for an ICJ advisory opinion on climate obligations?
2. What questions has the ICJ been requested to advise on?
3. What impacts do the authors believe an ICJ opinion could have?

The United Nations has just backed a landmark resolution on climate justice.

Last week, the U.N. General Assembly supported a Pacific-led resolution asking the International Court of Justice (ICJ) to provide an advisory opinion on a country's climate obligations.

This has been hailed as a "turning point in climate justice" and a victory for the Pacific youth who spearheaded the campaign.

But what does this U.N. decision actually mean? Does an advisory opinion from the ICJ have any teeth? And what might be the legal consequences for rich countries, like Australia, that have contributed the most to the climate problem?

What Is an ICJ Advisory Opinion?

The ICJ is the world court and the leading global authority on international law. It generally hears disputes between countries known as "contentious cases" such as the 2010 case brought by Australia against Japan over whaling in the Southern Ocean. In that case, the court ruled in Australia's favour.

However, the ICJ can also issue advisory opinions. This is a kind of general advice on the status of international law on a particular topic. Opinions must be requested by one of the organs or specialised agencies of the U.N., such as the General Assembly.

On March 29 2023, the U.N. General Assembly resolved to seek an ICJ advisory opinion on the obligations of states with respect to climate change. That was based on draft text put forward by the tiny Pacific nation of Vanuatu.

Significantly, this resolution was co-sponsored by 105 states, including Australia. It's the first time the General Assembly has requested an advisory opinion from the ICJ with unanimous state support.

The question put to the ICJ asks whether countries have an obligation to protect the global climate system. It also seeks advice on the "legal consequences" when countries' actions or omissions cause significant climate harm to small island states and future generations in particular.

The U.N. will communicate the resolution to the ICJ in coming weeks and the court will then organise hearings over the next few months. It's expected an advisory opinion will be issued six to 12 months later.

A Win for the Pacific

The adoption of the advisory opinion resolution represents an important milestone in a long-running fight by Pacific small island nations and youth activists to secure climate justice.

For these communities, climate change is already causing or exacerbating harm to natural and human systems. Indeed, only a few weeks before the U.N. General Assembly decision, a rare double cyclone event ripped through Vanuatu.

Faced with these threats, Pacific nations like Tuvalu and Palau have previously publicly discussed options for seeking a ruling from the ICJ. These efforts met with stiff resistance from major emitting countries, which eventually saw the proposals shelved.

Renewed efforts began in 2019 with 27 law students from The University of the South Pacific forming Pacific Islands Students Fighting Climate Change.

The students worked with the Vanuatu government to launch a new campaign for a General Assembly resolution on climate change and human rights. Introducing the resolution, Vanuatu's prime minister Ishmael Kalsakau stated:

> This is not a silver bullet, but it can make an important contribution to climate action, including by catalysing much higher ambition under the Paris Agreement.

For student campaigners like Cynthia Houniuhi, it means

> an opportunity to do something bigger than ourselves, bigger than our fears.

What Might the ICJ Advisory Opinion Deliver?

Advisory opinions issued by the ICJ are—as the name suggests—advisory. They are not legally binding on any country or on the General Assembly. So this climate advisory opinion will not establish the accountability of particular countries for climate harms, nor deliver compensation to vulnerable nations like Vanuatu.

Nonetheless, the authority of the world court means its advisory opinions do matter in shaping how countries understand their international obligations.

There is an opportunity with this opinion to cement emerging links between climate harms and human rights, which could open up new avenues for litigation either domestically or internationally. Already there are several new climate rights cases underway, with the European Court of Human Rights hearing its first two climate cases (against Switzerland and France) on the same day the advisory opinion resolution was adopted.

The ICJ opinion could also provide an extra incentive for countries to reexamine and strengthen their national emissions reduction targets, to make sure they are compliant with the Paris Agreement. As the new fund for climate-related loss and damage takes shape at this year's international climate meeting (COP28 in Dubai), negotiators may be thinking about how the rules they are crafting could complement the ICJ opinion.

Australia's support signals our government understands the need to strengthen cooperation and solidarity in the region. Such efforts—including increasing the ambition of Australia's emissions reduction target and contributing funds to the emerging loss and damage fund—would be tangible indications Australia is striving to meet its international obligations. It's about being a good neighbor while also avoiding future lawsuits.

Periodical and Internet Sources Bibliography

The following articles have been selected to supplement the diverse views presented in this chapter.

Mohamed Adow, "Climate Debt: What the West Owes the Rest," *Foreign Affairs*, May/June 2020. https://www.foreignaffairs.com/articles/world/2020-04-13/climate-debt.

Gregory Barber, "Climate Justice Is Possible—Just Look Beyond Technology," *Wired*, September 29, 2022. https://www.wired.com/story/rewired-2022-technology-climate-justice-community-policy/.

Zack Colman, "Justice or Overreach?: As Crucial Test Looms, Big Greens Are Under Fire." *Politico*, June 19, 2022. https://www.politico.com/news/2022/06/19/big-green-justice-environment-00040148.

Sonja Klinsky, "Climate Change Is a Justice Issue: These Six Charts Show Why," the Conversation, November 3, 2021. https://theconversation.com/climate-change-is-a-justice-issue-these-6-charts-show-why-170072.

Stephan Lezak, "Giving Up on Limiting Warming to 1.5 Degrees Celsius Is a Luxury Only the Rich Can Afford," the *New Republic*, November 22, 2022. https://newrepublic.com/article/169047/warming-two-degrees-celsius-climate.

Joe McCarthy, "Why Climate Change and Poverty Are Inextricably Linked," Global Citizen, February 19, 2020. https://www.globalcitizen.org/en/content/climate-change-is-connected-to-poverty/.

Bill McKibben, "Why the World's Rich Nations Must Pay for Climate Damage," YaleEnvironment360, October 14, 2021. https://e360.yale.edu/features/for-climate-equity-developing-nations-must-be-paid-for-damages.

Robin Rose Parker, "Climate Change and Environmental Justice are Inextricably Linked," *Washington Post*, June 14, 2022. https://www.washingtonpost.com/magazine/2022/06/14/climate-justice-green-new-deal/.

Brad Plumer, Lisa Friedman, Max Bearak, and Jenny Gross, "In a First, Rich Countries Agree to Pay for Climate Damages in Poor

Nations, *New York Times*, November 19, 2022. https://www.nytimes.com/2022/11/19/climate/un-climate-damage-cop27.html.

Kevin D. Williamson, "An 'Ecosocialist' Heard From," the *National Review*, October 11, 2018. https://www.nationalreview.com/2018/10/ecosocialist-climate-change-meets-socialism/.

OPPOSING VIEWPOINTS® SERIES

CHAPTER 3

Has the Media Made Climate Change More Politically Polarizing?

Chapter Preface

There is a huge amount of science on climate change and global warming. But for the most part, the only way the public can learn about that science is through the media. Sadly, the media hasn't always done a great job of keeping the public informed and educated about this issue. In this chapter, the authors dig into the problem of media coverage of climate change. Some argue that journalists are faced with some ethical dilemmas—or so it sometimes seems—when it comes to writing about climate activism and climate change. Still, that does not give them an excuse for their failures. Others pin the blame on the public, pointing out that journalists have been writing about climate change for a century; the public just hasn't paid attention, or hasn't believed what it was hearing.

When it comes to believing in climate change, the problem is a glut of misinformation, say some of the authors in this chapter. The public are being fed inaccuracies and lies, and the media is not doing enough to provide accurate information to counter that. Media outlets, keen to be seen as fair and presenting both sides of the issue, have contributed to the problem by giving equal time to fringe views, non-experts, and outright quacks—a fallacy called "bothsidesism." Others say that the professional media is not the biggest part of the problem. Instead, social media claims the brunt of the responsibility by providing a largely unregulated stream of unvetted statements, and both deliberate and inadvertent misinformation.

Where does the misinformation start? For the most part, it starts with oil companies, whose scientists were among the first to discover that climate change was real, posed a grave threat, and was caused by human activities. Yet these companies deliberately hid the evidence and worked to seed doubt about the science and confuse the public about this crucial issue.

VIEWPOINT 1

> "Why has it taken so long for the warnings in the article to be heard—and acted on?"

The Media Has Covered Climate Change for More than 100 Years

Linden Ashcroft

In this viewpoint, Linden Ashcroft points out that the media has been covering climate change for more than 100 years. The problem, she writes, is not with the amount of coverage, but the nature of it. Groups funded by the fossil fuel industry seeded skepticism about established science in order to allow the industry to continue operating, and the media gave space to skeptics in the name of "balance." However, in recent years there has been a decline in climate change denial and skepticism, which is a promising sign. Linden Ashcroft is a lecturer in climate science and science communication at the University of Melbourne in Australia.

As you read, consider the following questions:

1. When was the greenhouse effect first demonstrated, according to Ashcroft?
2. Who funded the efforts to create doubt about climate change science?

"For 110 Years, Climate Change Has Been in the News. Are We Finally Ready to Listen?" by Linden Ashcroft, The Conversation, August 15, 2022. https://theconversation.com/for-110-years-climate-change-has-been-in-the-news-are-we-finally-ready-to-listen-188646. Licensed under CC BY 4.0 International.

3. How has public opinion about climate change evolved in recent years, according to this viewpoint?

On August 14, 1912, a small New Zealand newspaper published a short article announcing global coal usage was affecting our planet's temperature.

This piece from 110 years ago is now famous, shared across the internet this time every year as one of the first pieces of climate science in the media (even though it was actually a reprint of a piece published in a New South Wales mining journal a month earlier).

So how did it come about? And why has it taken so long for the warnings in the article to be heard—and acted on?

The Fundamental Science Has Been Understood for a Long Time

American scientist and women's rights campaigner Eunice Foote is now widely credited as being the first person to demonstrate the greenhouse effect back in 1856, several years before United Kingdom researcher John Tyndall published similar results.

Her rudimentary experiments showed carbon dioxide and water vapor can absorb heat, which, scaled up, can affect the temperature of the earth. We've therefore known about the relationship between greenhouse gases and Earth's temperature for at least 150 years.

Four decades later, Swedish scientist Svente Arrhenius did some basic calculations to estimate how much the Earth's temperature would change if we doubled the amount of CO_2 in the atmosphere. At the time, the CO_2 levels were around 295 parts per million molecules of air. This year, we've hit 421 parts per million—more than 50% higher than pre-industrial times.

Arrhenius estimated doubling CO_2 would produce a world 5° hotter. This, thankfully, is higher than modern calculations but not too far off, considering he wasn't using a sophisticated computer model! At the time, the Swede was more worried about moving into a new ice age than global warming, but by the 1900s he was startling his classes with news the world was slowly warming due to the burning of coal.

Climate Science Began on the Fringe

The 1912 New Zealand snippet was likely based on a four-page spread from Popular Mechanics magazine, which drew from the work of Arrhenius and others.

When climate advocates point to articles like this and say we knew about climate change, this overlooks the fact Arrhenius' ideas were generally considered fringe, meaning not many people took them seriously. In fact, there was backlash about how efficient carbon dioxide actually was as a greenhouse gas.

When the first world war began, the topic lost momentum. Oil began its rise, pushing aside promising technologies such as electric cars—which in 1900 had a third of the fledgling U.S. car market—in favor of fossil-fuel technological developments and military goals. The idea humans could affect the whole planet remained on the fringe.

The Callendar Effect

It wasn't until the 1930s that human-induced climate change resurfaced. U.K. engineer Guy Callendar put together weather observations from around the world and found temperatures had already increased.

Not only was Callendar the first to clearly identify a warming trend and connect it to changes in atmospheric carbon dioxide, he also teased apart the importance of CO_2 compared to water vapor, another potent greenhouse gas.

Just like the 1912 article, Callendar also underestimated the rate of warming we would see in the 80 years after his first results. He predicted the world would be only 0.39° hotter by the year 2000, rather than the 1° we observed. However it did get the attention of researchers, sparking intense scientific debate.

But at the end of the 1930s, the world went to war once more. Callendar's discoveries swiftly took a backseat to battles, and rebuilding.

The Politics of Climate

Fresh Hope Scuttled by Merchants of Doubt

In 1957, scientists began the International Geophysical Year—an intense investigation of the Earth and its poles and atmosphere. This saw the creation of the atmospheric monitoring stations tracking our steady increase in human-caused greenhouse gases. At the same time, oil companies were becoming aware of the impact their business was having on the Earth.

During these post-war decades, there was little political polarisation over climate. Margaret Thatcher—hardly a raging leftie—saw global warming as a clear threat during her time as U.K. prime minister. In 1988, NASA scientist James Hansen gave

JUST 10 PUBLISHERS ARE BEHIND 69 PERCENT OF CLIMATE CHANGE MISINFORMATION ON FACEBOOK

As the U.N. climate conference (COP26) aims to find "the world's last best chance" to curb greenhouse gas emissions, 10 publishers including Breitbart, Russia Today, and Media Research Center are responsible for spreading most climate change misinformation on Facebook, according to a new report by U.K.-based Center for Countering Digital Hate (CCDH).

The 10 fringe publishers, titled "The Toxic Ten," are fuelling 69 percent of digital climate change denial content on Facebook.

The science is undeniable and human activity is warming our planet at an ever-accelerating rate and leading to catastrophic climate change, it said.

"Yet, 10 publishers—'The Toxic Ten'—are spreading baseless, unscientific climate denial on their own websites and across social media," the CCDH said in a statement.

"It's a climate denial propaganda machine funded in part by Google via ad revenue, and spread across the world via social media, in particular Facebook, who allow them to pay to promote their denial," the Center added.

Meta, Facebook's parent company, disputed the CCDH findings.

his now famous address to the U.S. Congress claiming global warming had already arrived.

Momentum was growing. Many conservationists were encouraged by the Montreal Protocol, which more or less halted the use of ozone-depleting substances to tackle the growing hole in the ozone layer. Surely we could do the same to stop climate change?

As we now know, we didn't. Phasing out a class of chemicals was one thing. But to wean ourselves off the fossil fuels on which the modern world was built? Much harder.

Climate change became politicised, with conservative pro-business parties around the world adopting climate scepticism.

> "The 700,000 interactions this report says were on climate denial represent 0.3 percent of the over 200 million interactions on English public climate change content from Pages and public groups over the same time period," according to a Meta spokesperson, Engadget reported.
>
> In an interview with *The Washington Post*, Imran Ahmed, the chief executive of the CCDH, said the organisation looked at nearly 7,000 articles published between October 2020 and October 2021.
>
> He called the sample "robust" and said there was enough data "to derive representative finds of trends."
>
> The CCDH report claimed that eight of the companies in "The Toxic Ten" made $5.3 million in Google ad revenue over the last six months.
>
> "We are calling on Facebook and Google to stop promoting and funding climate denial, start labelling it as misinformation, and stop giving the advantages of their enormous platforms to lies and misinformation," the Center emphasised.
>
> More than 100 heads of state and government are deliberating at COP26 and over the coming days, negotiators will continue working towards a formal outcome on November 12.
>
> In March this year, another CCDH report had found that as much as 73 percent of vaccine misinformation on Facebook can be linked to only 12 individuals, dubbed as the "disinformation dozen."

"10 publishers behind 69% climate change misinformation on Facebook," The Shillong Times, November 4, 2021.

Global media coverage often included a sceptic in the interests of "balance." This, in turn, made many people believe the jury was still out—when the science was becoming ever more certain and alarming.

With this scepticism came delays. The 1992 Kyoto Protocol aimed at reducing greenhouse gases took until 2005 to be ratified. Science—and scientists themselves—came under attack. Soon a vicious tussle was underway, with loud voices—often funded by fossil fuel interests—questioning overwhelming scientific evidence.

Sadly for us, these noisy efforts worked to slow action. People refusing to accept the science bought the fossil fuel industry at least another decade, even as climate change continued to increase, with supercharged natural disasters and intensifying heatwaves.

The Best Time to Act Was 1912. The Next Best Time Is Now

After decades of setbacks, climate science and social movements are now louder than ever in calling for strong and meaningful action.

The science is beyond doubt. While the first Intergovernmental Panel on Climate Change report in 1990 stated global warming "could be largely due to natural variability", the latest from 2021 states humans have "unequivocally […] warmed the atmosphere, ocean and land."

We've even seen a welcome change in previously sceptical media outlets. And as we saw at May's federal election, public opinion is on the side of the planet.

National and international climate policies are stronger than ever, and although there is still much more to be done, it finally seems that government, business and public sentiment are moving in the same direction.

Let's use the 110th anniversary of this short snippet as a reminder to keep speaking up and pushing, finally, for the change we must have.

VIEWPOINT 2

> "Selective failure of quality control and editorial responsibility when it comes to climate change presents a grave public disservice."

The Media Gets Climate Change Wrong

Stephan Lewandowsky and Michael Ashley

The previous viewpoint holds the public responsible for at least some climate change misinformation. Here, the authors zero in on the press, listing several mistakes the media makes when it comes to climate change coverage. By creating the narrative that there is a debate around climate change rather than acknowledging that climate change is a fact, the media has legitimized climate change denial. In this sense, it has played a harmful role in public and political conversations on climate change. Stephan Lewandowsky is a cognitive scientist at the University of Bristol in the U.K. Michael Ashley is a professor of astrophysics at the University of New South Wales in Sydney, Australia.

As you read, consider the following questions:

1. What analogy do the authors make between climate change and gravity?

"The False, the Confused and the Mendacious: How the Media Gets It Wrong on Climate Change," by Stephan Lewandowsky and Michael Ashley, The Conversation, June 24, 2011. https://theconversation.com/the-false-the-confused-and-the-mendacious-how-the-media-gets-it-wrong-on-climate-change-1558. Licensed under CC BY 4.0 International.

2. What, according to Lewandowsky and Ashley, is the difference between a skeptic and a denier?
3. What is the difference between balance and impartiality? Why do the authors advocate impartiality and not balance?

Over the past two weeks The Conversation has highlighted the consensus of experts that climate change caused by humans is both real and poses a serious risk for the future.

We have also revealed the deep flaws in the conduct of so-called climate "sceptics" who largely operate outside the scientific context.

But to what extent is the "science settled"? Is there any possibility that the experts are wrong and the deniers are right?

Certainty in Science

If you ask a scientist whether something is "settled" beyond any doubt, they will almost always reply "no."

Nothing is 100% certain in science.

So how certain is climate science? Is there a 50% chance that the experts are wrong and that the climate within our lifetimes will be just fine? Or is there a 10% chance that the experts are wrong? Or 1%, or only 0.0001%?

The answer to these questions is vital because if the experts are right, then we must act to avert a major risk.

Dropping Your Phone

Suppose that you lose your grip on your phone. Experience tells us that the phone will fall to the ground.

You drop a phone, it falls down.

Fact.

Science tells us that this is due to gravity, and no one doubts its inevitability.

However, while science has a good understanding of gravity, our knowledge is only partial. In fact, physicists know that at a very deep level our theory of gravity is inconsistent with quantum mechanics, so one or both will have to be modified.

We simply don't know for sure how gravity works.

But we still don't jump off bridges, and you would be pretty silly to drop your phone onto a concrete floor in the hope that gravity is wrong.

Climate Change vs. Gravity: Greater Complexity, Comparable Certainty

Our predictions of climate change aren't as simple as the action of gravity on a dropped phone.

The Earth is a very complex system: there are natural effects like volcanoes, and variations in the sun; there are the vagaries of the weather; there are complicating factors such as clouds, and how ice responds; and then there are the human influences such as deforestation and CO_2 emissions.

But despite these complexities, some aspects of climate science are thoroughly settled.

We know that atmospheric CO_2 is increasing due to humans. We know that this CO_2, while being just a small fraction of the atmosphere, has an important influence on temperature.

We can calculate the effect, and predict what is going to happen to the earth's climate during our lifetimes, all based on fundamental physics that is as certain as gravity.

The consensus opinion of the world's climate scientists is that climate change is occurring due to human CO_2 emissions. The changes are rapid and significant, and the implications for our civilization may be dire. The chance of these statements being wrong is vanishingly small.

Skepticism and Denialism

Some people will be understandably skeptical about that last statement. But when they read up on the science, and have their questions answered by climate scientists, they come around.

These people are true skeptics, and a degree of skepticism is healthy.

Other people will disagree with the scientific consensus on climate change, and will challenge the science on internet blogs and opinion pieces in the media, but no matter how many times they are shown to be wrong, they will never change their opinions.

These people are deniers.

The recent articles in The Conversation have put the deniers under the microscope. Some readers have asked us in the comments to address the scientific questions that the deniers bring up.

This has been done.

Not once. Not twice. Not 10 times. Probably more like 100 or 1,000 times.

Denier arguments have been dealt with by scientists, again and again and again.

But like zombies, the deniers keep coming back with the same long-falsified and nonsensical arguments.

The deniers have seemingly endless enthusiasm to post on blogs, write letters to editors, write opinion pieces for newspapers, and even publish books. What they rarely do is write coherent scientific papers on their theories and submit them to scientific journals. The few published papers that have been skeptical about climate change have not withstood the test of time.

The Phony Debate on Climate Change

So if the evidence is this strong, why is there resistance to action on climate change in Australia?

At least two reasons can be cited.

First, as The Conversation has revealed, there are a handful of individuals and organizations who, by avoiding peer review, have engineered a phony public debate about the science, when in fact that debate is absent from the one arena where our scientific knowledge is formed.

These individuals and organizations have so far largely escaped accountability.

But their free ride has come to an end, as the next few weeks on The Conversation will continue to show. The second reason, alas, involves systemic failures by the media.

Systemic media failures arise from several presumptions about the way science works, which range from being utterly false to dangerously ill-informed to overtly malicious and mendacious.

The False

Let's begin with what is merely false. A tacit presumption of many in the media and the public is that climate science is a brittle house of cards that can be brought down by a single new finding or the discovery of a single error.

Nothing could be further from the truth. Climate science is a cumulative enterprise built upon hundreds of years of research. The heat-trapping properties of CO_2 were discovered in the middle of the 19th century, pre-dating even Sherlock Holmes and Queen Victoria.

The resulting robust knowledge will not be overturned by a single new finding.

A further false presumption of the media is that scientific opinions must somehow be balanced by an opposing view. While balance is an appropriate conversational frame for the political sphere, it is wholly inappropriate for scientific issues, where what matters is the balance of evidence, not opinion.

At first glance, one might be tempted to forgive the media's inappropriate inclusion of unfounded contrarian opinions, given that its function is to stimulate broad debate in which, ideally, even exotic opinions are given a voice.

But the media by and large do not report the opinions of 9/11 "truthers" who think that the attacks were an "inside job" of the Bush administration. The media also do not report the opinion of people who believe Prince Phillip runs the world's drug trade. The fact that equally outlandish pseudo-scientific nonsense about climate science can be sprouted on TV by a cat palmist is evidence not of an obsession with balance but of a striking and selective failure of editorial responsibility.

What is needed instead of the false symmetry implied by "balance" is what the BBC calls impartiality—fact-based reporting that evaluates the evidence and comes to a reality-based conclusion.

The Dangerously Ill-Formed

An example of a dangerously ill-informed opinion on how science works is the widely propagated myth that scientists somehow have a "vested interest," presumably financial, in climate change. This myth has been carefully crafted by deniers to create a chimerical symmetry between their own ties to political and economic interests and the alleged "vested interests" of scientists.

In actual fact, climate scientists have as much vested interest in the existence of climate change as cancer researchers do in the existence of the human papilloma virus (HPV).

Cancer researchers are motivated by the fact that cervical cancer kills, and the scientists who developed the HPV vaccine did so to save lives, not to get their grants renewed.

Climate scientists are likewise motivated by the fact that climate change kills 140,000 people per year right at this very moment, according to the World Health Organization.

The scientists who have been alerting the public of this risk for nearly 20 years did so to save lives, not to get their grants renewed.

Climate scientists are being motivated by the realization that humanity has got itself into serious trouble with climate change, and it will need the best scientific advice to navigate a solution.

As scientists, we ask not for special consideration by the media, but simply for the same editorial responsibility and quality control that is routinely applied to all other arenas of public discourse.

Selective failure of quality control and editorial responsibility when it comes to climate change presents a grave public disservice.

The Malicious

Finally, no truthful analysis of the Australian media landscape can avoid highlighting the maliciousness of some media organizations, primarily those owned by Newscorp, which are cartoonish in their brazen serial distortion of scientists and scientific findings.

Those organizations have largely escaped accountability to date, and we believe that it is a matter of urgency to expose their practice.

For example, it is not a matter of legitimate editorial process to misrepresent what experts are telling Newscorp reporters—some of whom have been known to apologize to scientists in advance and off the record for their being tasked to return from public meetings, not with an actual news story but with scathing statements from the handful of deniers in the audience.

It is not a matter of legitimate editorial process to invert the content of scientific papers.

It is not a matter of legitimate editorial process to misrepresent what scientists say.

It is not a matter of legitimate editorial process to prevent actual scientists from setting the record straight after the science has been misrepresented.

None of those sadly common actions are compatible with legitimate journalistic ethics, and they should have no place in a knowledge economy of the 21st century.

The very fact that society is wracked by a phony debate where there is none in the scientific literature provides strong evidence that the Australian media has tragically and thoroughly failed the Australian public.

VIEWPOINT 3

> "People need more guidance on how to effectively spot misinformation, and how to find reliable information about climate change."

Climate Change Misinformation Fools Too Many People

Mikey Biddlestone and Sander van der Linden

This viewpoint by Mikey Biddlestone and Sander van der Linden is an analysis of surveys about climate change and the media in the U.K. The authors found that too many people fall for misinformation about global warming. However, they also propose solutions to this problem to help the public be better informed on climate change. At the time this viewpoint was published, Mikey Biddlestone was a post-doctoral research assistant in the Social Decision Making Lab at the University of Cambridge. Sander van der Linden is a professor of social psychology at Cambridge and director of the Social Decision Making Lab.

As you read, consider the following questions:

1. What is "pre-bunking," and how do the authors compare that to vaccinations?

"Climate Change Misinformation Fools Too Many People – but There Are Ways to Combat It," by Mikey Biddlestone and Sander van der Linden, The Conversation, October 28, 2021. https://theconversation.com/climate-change-misinformation-fools-too-many-people-but-there-are-ways-to-combat-it-170658. Licensed under CC BY 4.0 International.

2. What can scientists do to help, according to these authors?
3. What can the media do to help repair this damage?

In recent decades, people in the U.K. have watched climate change shift from being an abstract threat discussed on the news to an increasingly common presence in everyday life. As the frequency and intensity of heatwaves, floods and other extreme weather events has risen, so has public concern about climate change. A 2019 poll found 80% of people were fairly or very worried, while a more recent survey ranked climate change as the most important issue.

People are more engaged with the climate crisis than ever before. But how well do they understand it? And which sources of information do they trust the most? We wanted to understand where the public gets much of its information on the topic and what the most effective ways of keeping people informed are.

We surveyed more than 1,700 adults living in the U.K. and found that almost half the sample were unable to correctly identify 50% of fake climate change news headlines, and almost half (44%) of all respondents were unaware of how often they encountered misinformation online. These numbers suggest that people need more guidance on how to effectively spot misinformation, and how to find reliable information about climate change.

What We Found

Working with YouGov and The Conversation, we asked 1,722 people to read five real and four fake news headlines about climate change. Almost half (46%) mistakenly believed that "Scientists disagree on the cause of climate change" and 35% incorrectly thought that "Scientists believe the Sun has impacted the Earth's rise in temperature."

However, a majority of respondents also correctly identified fake headlines such as "Carbon dioxide levels are tiny. They can't make a difference" (70%) and "Melting an ice cube in a measuring cup full of water doesn't raise the water level, so melting icebergs cannot raise sea levels" (68%).

Over half of respondents correctly guessed the real headlines "More than one million species are at risk of extinction by climate change" (65%), "Earth had its second warmest year in recorded history in 2019" (62%), and "The worst impacts of climate change could be irreversible by 2030" (55%).

But only 15% knew that "Switching to jet fuel made from mustard plants would reduce carbon emissions by nearly 70%" was false, and only 34% were right in thinking that "Enough ice melted on a single day to cover Florida in two inches of water."

We also asked people how much trust they had in certain sources of climate change information. While online influencers (6%), social media outlets (7%), tabloid newspapers (13%), politicians (20%), journalists (30%), broadsheet newspapers (37%), and broadcast media outlets (38%) were among the least trusted sources, the vast majority trusted academics (67%) and their own friends and family (59%) to convey information about climate change that was trustworthy.

A majority of those we surveyed thought accurate reporting was important, with 78% saying that climate change misinformation is very or fairly damaging to efforts to tackle the climate crisis.

When asked about media coverage of climate change, 39% claimed that media reporting overall was too abstract, with excessive focus on the future rather than the issues of today. Similarly, 29% thought media coverage was confusing, citing too many conflicting opinions (55%) and a distrust of politicians (55%) and news outlets (54%).

Finally, the majority of respondents (59%) were worried about climate change, with an even larger majority (80%) reporting a general willingness to make relevant lifestyle changes to stem the crisis.

What This Means

Despite widespread awareness of the problems caused by fake news, many people we surveyed didn't recognise their own role in this process. While large majorities worried about the effects of climate change misinformation and said that they didn't share it themselves, 24% reported hardly ever fact-checking the information they read.

This could suggest the public aren't sure which sources are reliable, making them more vulnerable to the very misinformation they see as damaging to the cause of tackling climate change.

Clearly, more can be done to educate people on how to distinguish real from fake climate change information. One way to do this is through a process called inoculation, or prebunking.

Just as vaccines train cells to detect foreign invaders, research has shown that stories which pre-emptively refute short extracts of misinformation can help readers develop mental antibodies that allow them to detect misinformation on their own in the future. Recent work has even used games to help people detect the larger strategies that are used to spread misinformation about climate change.

Although social media companies such as Facebook have started to debunk climate myths on their platform, politicians and social media outlets appear to have an untrustworthy reputation. This was not the case for sources with perceived expertise on the topic, such as scientists. We therefore recommend that the trust held towards experts should be harnessed, by more frequently disseminating their views on social media and in traditional media outlets.

In our survey, only 21% of people understood that between 90% and 100% of climate scientists have concluded that humans are causing climate change (99% according to a recent paper). Decades-long campaigns by fossil fuel companies have sought to cast doubt on the scientific consensus. Media messages should therefore continue to communicate the overwhelming scientific consensus on climate change.

Through years of research on the topic, we have identified several ingredients for trustworthy science communication. These include prebunking myths and falsehoods, reliably informing people (don't persuade), offering balance but not false balance (highlight the weight of evidence or scientific consensus), verifying the quality of the underlying evidence, and explaining sources of uncertainty. If communicators want to earn people's trust, they need to start by displaying trustworthy behaviour.

VIEWPOINT 4

> *"The fossil fuel industry's current strategy is to encourage disagreement about these facts as a means to foster division."*

Climate Misinformation on Social Media Is Undermining Climate Action

Jeff Turrentine

While other viewpoints in this chapter have looked at media such as newspapers, periodicals, and television, this viewpoint by Jeff Turrentine focuses on social media, where, the author argues, fossil fuel interests have turned their efforts to seed doubt about climate change. The author considers the particular characteristics of social media that make it susceptible to climate misinformation and whether it is possible to combat this misinformation. He also considers the question of whether social media platforms have attempted to respond to this and whether they have a responsibility to do so. Jeff Turrentine is culture and politics columnist for onEarth, a publication of the Natural Resources Defense Council.

As you read, consider the following questions:

1. How are the efforts of the fossil fuel industry to undermine climate action similar to efforts by the tobacco

"Climate Misinformation on Social Media Is Undermining Climate Action," by Jeff Turrentine, Natural Resources Defense Council, April 19, 2022. Reprinted by permission.

industry to deny the health risks of cigarettes, according to this viewpoint?
2. Why is social media such a fruitful place for spreading climate misinformation, according to Turrentine?
3. How have social media companies responded to the problem?

To hear some climate scientists and activists tell it, there are actually encouraging signs that climate skepticism is on the decline. The evidence for climate change that's all around us—temperatures in Antarctica were recently 70 degrees Fahrenheit warmer than they're supposed to be—has made it harder and harder for deniers to, well, deny.

But fossil fuel interests can't afford to let public opinion settle on the side of science. And so, with their profit margins very much on the line, these interests have replaced outright denial with spreading climate misinformation meant to undermine climate science and solutions. Their aim is to sow enough doubt to delay real climate action.

Unfortunately, our current social media ecosystem makes doing so all too easy.

What Exactly Is Climate Misinformation?

Misinformation is just what it sounds like: the sharing of information that is false or incorrect. When someone deliberately spreads misinformation with the intent to mislead, we call it disinformation. Much of this intentionally misleading content about climate change or renewable energy is funded by a handful of industries, particularly the fossil fuel industry, and often conceived by conservative think tanks and front groups. Then various "influencers" like these help amplify it.

The average individuals who end up resharing this content aren't necessarily trying to mislead; they may feel like they're merely "asking questions," or that they've happened upon an underreported news story worth passing along. By this point, the distinction between disinformation and misinformation can be almost nonexistent. What's important to fossil fuel interests is that the information is out there, circulating.

Why Does the Spread of Climate Misinformation Matter?

Every falsehood, distortion, and conspiracy theory about climate change is an obstacle to meaningful climate action—which is a collective effort that requires our agreement on a set of basic facts. The fossil fuel industry's current strategy is to encourage disagreement about these facts as a means to foster division. And research has shown it works, contributing to everything from political inaction to the rejection of mitigation policies. Of course, the fossil fuel industry expected that. Spreading misinformation on social media is just a mutation of what they've done offline for decades. It's also a page right out of the tobacco industry's playbook. A comprehensive 2020 report on climate misinformation quoted language from a memo by a tobacco-industry executive explaining how the same tactics were employed during that industry's decades-long attempt to suppress the impact of scientific studies linking cigarettes to cancer: "Doubt is our product, since it is the best means of competing with the 'body of fact' that exists in the minds of the general public. It is also the means of establishing a controversy."

How Does It Play Out Online?

Fossil fuel companies, other major polluters, and their allies have spent hundreds of millions of dollars to spread false and misleading content on social media. One analysis found that 16 of the world's biggest polluters were responsible for placing more than 1,700 of these ads on Facebook in 2021. Collectively, those ads garnered roughly 150 million impressions and have earned nearly $5 million for the platform.

Clean energy is a favorite target of these 21st-century social media merchants of doubt. For example, the Texas Public Policy

Foundation, a think tank with strong ties to the oil and gas industry, has inserted itself into regional conflicts over wind energy by making YouTube videos framing these battles as clashes between local, small business Davids against multinational, clean energy Goliaths. Last fall, ExxonMobil paid for at least 350 ads intended to influence proposed legislation in New York state that would phase out natural gas in new buildings. And knowing that users are far more likely to trust political information that appears to be coming from grassroots organizations over information that is clearly identifiable as corporate advertising, oil and gas companies have become skilled at fabricating front groups that look, sound, and act like nationwide collections of "concerned" citizens. (Spoiler alert: They are not.)

Climate misinformation has even been incorporated into the marketing plans to help sell the public on the continued use of fossil fuels. Trade groups for the natural gas industry have actually paid Instagram influencers—often young women with large followings among foodies and cooking enthusiasts—to talk up the benefits of cooking on a gas stove as opposed to an electric one, in an effort to make the burning of this particular fossil fuel seem like a requirement for successful recipe outcomes.

Much of this overall messaging is often reinforced by the biggest individual spreaders of misinformation online, some of whom receive funding from fossil fuel interest groups.

What Makes Social Media the Perfect Breeding Ground?

Researchers at Indiana University have identified three separate but interrelated kinds of bias that, in their words, "make the social media ecosystem vulnerable to both intentional and accidental misinformation."

Cognitive biases are systematic errors in thinking that stem from our propensity to use mental shortcuts. Social bias is the tendency to trust information that comes from people you know (or with whom you identify) over information from other sources.

And algorithmic bias comes courtesy of social media platforms themselves: Sites like Facebook and Twitter tailor the content that you see every day based on what they predict you'll react to most passionately—whether your reaction is one of joy, sympathy, or anger.

Together, this is basically a recipe for discourse disaster. Cognitive bias means we're much more likely to believe—and share—information that sounds true to us without taking the time to confirm whether it is, indeed, true. Social bias means that we're even more likely to believe and share that information if it has come to us via someone in our social (or ideological) circle. And algorithmic bias means that once we've liked and shared this bit of maybe-true, maybe-not-true information, we're going to be seeing a lot more posts in the same vein.

Add to this the tiny yet significant dopamine rush that people experience from having others like and/or share their posts, and you essentially have a machine built for unfettered, unfiltered messaging. If you're an oil and gas executive or think tank analyst bent on killing clean energy, you couldn't devise a better means of getting the word out—and making it stick.

How Have Social Media Platforms Responded?

Social media sites have been rife with climate and clean energy misinformation for years—and their responses to this growing problem have been unsatisfyingly mixed, at best. After one research organization found that Twitter had allowed nearly half a million posts that deny climate change to appear on its platform in 2020, the site added a new climate change topic in order to steer activity toward scientifically accurate sources. It has also tweaked its algorithms to direct users toward credible information before they encounter misinformation, a strategy known as "pre-bunking."

In October, YouTube's parent company, Google, announced that the popular video site would no longer allow creators to earn money from content that "contradicts well-established scientific consensus around the existence and causes of climate change."

That hasn't put an end to misleading or deceptive content on these platforms, however. (For proof, just type the words "climate change hoax" into the platforms' search bars and see what comes up.)

Last year, Facebook—the world's most visited social media platform—announced that it would begin attaching warning labels to certain content and directing readers to a "climate science information center" containing accurate information. But a report issued in February from a watchdog group found that Facebook had in fact "fail[ed] to label half of the posts promoting articles from leading publishers of climate denial." That came on the heels of damning congressional testimony from ex-Facebook employee–turned–whistleblower Frances Haugen, who revealed that her former employer intentionally misled the public, including potential investors, about its efforts to fight climate misinformation.

One potential bright spot might be the response by Pinterest, which recently announced it would ban all climate misinformation from posts and ads.

What—If Anything—Can We Do About the Problem?

Congressional Republicans and Democrats have come together at different points to grill the CEOs of Facebook and Twitter about the negative impact their business practices have had on civil discourse. And though there has been some momentum in the direction of increased regulation, concerns about free speech—along with more practical concerns about the difficulty of fact-checking social information in real time—have hindered any real attempts to address the issue legislatively.

That pretty much leaves it up to us—social media users—to do a better job of separating online fact from online fiction. Fortunately, there are some tools at our disposal, which may be all we'll have for some time. After all, we've known for a minute now that misinformation, much like climate change, is a serious problem more broadly.

Right after the 2020 election, a CNN interviewer asked former president Barack Obama for his thoughts on why America seemed to be so divided along political and ideological lines. Almost without hesitation, Obama pointed to the power of our fractured media landscape to reinforce bias and give the patina of plausibility to untruths. "It's very hard for our democracy to function if we are operating on just completely different sets of facts," he said. Keep in mind, this sentence was uttered before the rise of the wholly unsubstantiated "Big Lie" promulgated by Donald Trump—that the 2020 presidential election was stolen from him through massive voter fraud—and before a not-insignificant number of Americans began rejecting the lifesaving COVID-19 vaccine based on fears that it might contain microchips.

To most of us, these are the symptoms of what President Obama, in a separate interview, deemed "an epistemological crisis." But to the merchants of climate and clean energy disinformation, they're welcome mats. If the good news is that more and more people are accepting the reality of climate change, despite decades' worth of attempts by fossil fuel interests to mislead us, the bad news is that these same interests have adopted a new tack. Social media is their secret weapon. And our current cultural proclivity for disagreement on nearly everything—including objective reality—is their strategic advantage.

VIEWPOINT 5

> *"The findings offer important insights into how science skeptics engage with and interpret news coverage of climate change."*

Changing the Language Used in Climate Coverage Can Help the Media Reach Climate Skeptics

Denise-Marie Ordway

In this viewpoint, Denise-Marie Ordway explains that though it likely is not possible to change the fact that the terms "climate change" and "global warning" have been politicized, newsrooms can encourage climate skeptics to be more open to engaging with the conversation by leaving out these terms and making other tweaks to the language used in these stories. Research conducted by Renita Coleman—a journalism professor at the University of Texas at Austin— and her team found that climate skeptics react hostilely to these terms and assume that the media is biased if they use them. However, through using language that comes across as more politically neutral, the researchers found that it is possible to reach climate skeptics. Denise-Marie Ordway is a writer for the Journalist's Resource of the Shorenstein Center at Harvard University.

"Want to Reach Skeptics? Researchers Suggesting Leaving the Term 'Climate Change' Out of Some News Coverage," by Denise-Marie Ordway, The Journalist's Resource, Shorenstein Center, May 28, 2022. https://journalistsresource.org/environment/science-skeptics-climate-change-news/. Licensed under CC BY-ND 4.0 International.

Has the Media Made Climate Change More Politically Polarizing?

As you read, consider the following questions:

1. What are the three changes the viewpoint suggests for climate change news coverage?
2. According to Renita Coleman, is it a violation of ethics to leave the causes of climate change out of coverage of climate change? Why or why not?
3. What makes words like "adapt" more appealing to skeptics in coverage of climate change?

If newsrooms want climate science skeptics to read and share news about climate change, researcher Renita Coleman recommends they do this: Leave the terms "climate change" and "global warming" out of their coverage.

"Research seems to indicate those are trigger words for skeptics," says Coleman, a journalism professor at the University of Texas at Austin. "This is what we found would trigger them to stop reading and instantly become hostile, [believing] 'Oh, that story is biased or that media organization is biased.'"

Coleman is the lead author of a new paper that investigates strategies to help journalists reach people who distrust science. She and her colleagues conducted an experiment that indicates small changes in how journalists cover climate change have the potential to elicit substantial changes in the way skeptics engage with the news.

In the experiment, after reading a news story that incorporated the three changes below, skeptics said they would likely seek out and share more news about climate change. They also said they would likely take steps to help mitigate its damage.

- Replacing "climate change" and "global warming" with the word "weather."
- Avoiding mentioning who or what causes climate change.
- Focusing heavily on solutions, or what the public can do to prepare for or adapt to the impacts of climate change.

Coleman says she's not suggesting journalists take this approach with all climate change stories. But they should consider doing it with some, she and her coauthors explain in "Reaching Science Skeptics: How Adaptive Framing of Climate Change Leads to Positive Responses Via Persuasion Knowledge and Perceived Behavioral Control," published May 19 in Communication Research.

The other researchers who worked on the study are Esther Thorson, a journalism professor at Michigan State University, and Cinthia Jimenez and Kami Vinton, two doctoral students at the University of Texas at Austin.

"It's not a violation of ethics by any means to not say anything about what causes climate change," explains Coleman, who, prior to entering academia, worked 15 years as a reporter, editor and designer at newspapers and magazines in Florida and North Carolina. "Every story has things that are left out, right? Leave this out occasionally. Not all the time—occasionally."

By making these changes, journalists might encourage many more people to read and share their work, she says.

"It's important to reach these people we're not reaching," she continues. "We're not going to turn people who don't believe climate change is man-made into believing. But we can get them to want to read more information and talk to other people about it versus shutting down."

To study the issue, Coleman and her fellow researchers recruited a sample of 1,200 U.S. adults and asked them to read a news article about climate change and then answer a series of questions. They made sure about half the people who participated were climate science skeptics.

The sample included individuals from various demographic backgrounds. Three-fourths were white, 13.1% were Black, 4.3% were Hispanic, 1.5% were Asian and 2.8% identified as "other." In terms of education, 43% had a high school education or less, 30% completed some college, 16% had a bachelor's degree and 11% had taken graduate-level courses or obtained a graduate degree.

The sample also represented different political ideologies. Almost 37% of participants identified as Democrats, 26.8% were Republican and 36.7% reported being Independents.

The authors recruited participants using Qualtrics, an organization that maintains a pool of people representing various demographic backgrounds who have agreed to complete online surveys. The researchers collected response data from Sept. 23, 2019 to Oct. 2, 2019.

For the experiment, Coleman created four news stories about climate change based on actual news coverage. Participants were randomly assigned to read one of them.

Two of the stories focused on high temperatures in Missouri. Two reported on ocean flooding in Orange County, California. Each story pair was visually similar — for example, the articles ran a page long, lacked photographs and purportedly came from The Associated Press. But they differed in terms of framing and word choices. One article in each pair blamed climate change and global warming while the other avoided those terms and emphasized solutions such as preparing for changes in weather and sea levels.

The headlines for each pair were worded differently:

Pair 1

Man-made global warming pushing ocean waters higher, experts say

Experts: Orange County towns must speed adaptation strategies for ocean's encroachment

Pair 2

With drought and heat waves ahead, Missouri grapples with impact of man-made climate change

Adaptation on the agenda as Missouri grapples with hotter future

After reading their assigned article, participants responded to online questions about the article and their responses to it. One question, for example, asked participants to rate how strongly they agreed or disagreed with statements such as "I was annoyed by

The Politics of Climate

the story because it seems to be trying to influence the audience" and "With this story's approach people can do something to stop damage from [the issue featured in the story]."

Another question asked participants about the likelihood they would take these future actions:

- "Endorse spending taxpayer money to address these issues in the ways described in this story."
- "Vote for elected officials who support this kind of planning."
- "Support efforts the story described to handle [the problem featured]."

After analyzing responses, the researchers realized that the framing and language of the news article did make a difference. "Removing any references to what causes climate change reduced perceptions that the news stories were trying to manipulate or persuade readers," they write.

They add that "removing any references to causes of climate change and emphasizing the ability to adapt increased the extent to which people considered themselves efficacious, responding more positively to ideas about working together to protect us all and stop damage, and that plans to adapt can work."

The authors also note the importance of "emphasizing the word 'adapt' and its derivatives, which implies adjusting, modifying, mitigating, and revising—all incremental changes that are easier to accomplish than fundamental, transformational change."

Other scholars have pointed out that the language journalists use—and the repetition of certain words and phrases—can influence audiences' interpretation of issues. Dietram Scheufele, the Taylor-Bascom Chair in Science Communication at the University of Wisconsin-Madison, said in a 2019 interview with The Journalist's Resource that "journalists have to be very careful, in terms of endorsing one term or the other."

Scheufele explained that in 2014, White House science adviser John Holdren pushed for a new term to describe the impact that rising levels of carbon dioxide and other greenhouse gases are having on the planet. Holden had argued "global climate disruption" captures the phenomena more accurately than do "global warming" and "climate change."

Coleman and her colleagues' work builds on earlier research that suggests avoiding the term "climate change" may help generate support for sending humanitarian aid to areas hit by natural disasters. Climate science skeptics who participated in that experiment "reported greater justifications for not helping the victims when the disaster was attributed to climate change," according to the paper, published in the journal Social Psychological and Personality Science in 2016.

Coleman, Thorson, Jimenez and Vinton note their study has several limitations. A big one: Their experiment involved only two story pairs.

"Climate change has many specific issues and future studies should create and test more stories on different climate topics," they write.

Also, their findings apply only to the sample of people who participated, not the U.S. public as a whole.

Even so, Coleman says, the findings offer important insights into how science skeptics engage with and interpret news coverage of climate change. Future research, she adds, could look at how skeptics respond to changes in the framing and language of stories about other contested topics.

Coleman and her colleagues have experimented with similar changes to news articles about vaccines and found that vaccine skeptics responded to the changes in ways similar to how climate science skeptics responded to changes in climate change coverage. The researchers presented their findings at a conference of the Association for Education in Journalism and Mass Communication in 2020.

As scholars continue investigating these issues, Coleman urges news outlets to consider what they might be doing to create a perception among some groups that they are trying to push their audiences to take a certain stance on an issue. Not everyone realizes how journalists do their work, she adds.

The Politics of Climate

"We are not [public relations] and we are not advertising, but that's not something people always get," she notes. "We need to think a little more nuanced, if you will, about what kinds of things we are doing to make people think we are trying to persuade them when we know we are not."

VIEWPOINT 6

> *"People respond well to two things: stories about what they can do, and how they can be part of a broader effective change. And those two things need to be connected."*

News Stories on Climate Change Need to Offer a More Optimistic Message

Jon Christensen

According to this viewpoint from Jon Christensen, the abundant news coverage of the potential catastrophic effects of climate change and the focus on how enough has not been done to stop these effects does have a purpose. This kind of news coverage makes the issue of climate change come across as appropriately urgent. However, these pessimistic and upsetting news stories do not compel people to action because they make the situation seem hopeless. Christensen asserts that there need to be more news stories about taking action and this action making a difference. While some people with extreme political beliefs will never support climate action, the vast majority of people can be reached by the right news stories. Jon Christensen is an adjunct assistant professor the Institute of the Environment and Sustainability, the department of history, and the Center for Digital Humanities at the University of California, Los Angeles.

"Climate Gloom and Doom? Bring It On. But We Need Stories About Taking Action, Too," by Jon Christensen, The Conversation, August 8, 2017. https://theconversation.com/climate-gloom-and-doom-bring-it-on-but-we-need-stories-about-taking-action-too-79464. Licensed under CC BY 4.0 International.

As you read, consider the following questions:

1. What does Christensen mean by "messengers matter"? What types of messengers does he think work well in climate stories?
2. What is negative spillover, and what is positive spillover?
3. According to Christensen, what are the characteristics shared by the most popular stories?

There's been no shortage of pessimistic news on climate change lately. A group of climate scientists and policy experts recently declared that we have just three years left to dramatically turn around carbon emissions, or else. Meanwhile a widely circulated New York magazine article detailed some of the most catastrophic possible consequences of climate change this century if we continue with business as usual.

Critics pounced on the article, claiming gloom-and-doom messages are disempowering and thus counterproductive.

But are they? And is there a better way to communicate to people about the urgency of climate change? In a somewhat unorthodox way—creating a mini-series of videos on climate change—my colleagues and I think we've gained some insight into these questions.

Communications: Art and Science

Naysayers to negative messaging miss an important function of this kind of apocalyptic thinking. It is useful in forcing us to imagine ourselves as the people who allowed a future we don't want to come about. In California, for example, Governor Jerry Brown has been a master of highlighting the existential threat of climate change. But his real genius has been linking that dystopian vision to what needs to be done to prevent it from becoming real. I call this approach "the California way: sunny with a chance of apocalypse."

Dystopian visions are easy to conjure these days; they come with scientific probabilities. The second part of that communication strategy—making a compelling connection to how we can act, individually and collectively, to avoid the worst consequences of climate change when so much of our lives depend on fossil fuels—is the really hard part.

To learn more about this challenge, we recently conducted a kind of real-life experiment in the art and science of climate communication with "Climate Lab," a series of six short, popular videos created by the University of California with Vox.

The series, which has had more than five million views and created a robust online discussion, grew out of a peer-reviewed report co-authored by 50 UC researchers entitled "Bending the Curve: Ten Scalable Solutions for Carbon Neutrality and Climate Stability." I was the senior editor, and we worked hard to make the executive summary a tool for communicating what needs to be done to get to carbon neutrality by midcentury. We wanted it to be used by UC President Janet Napolitano (who has pledged that the UC system will be carbon neutral by 2025), Governor Brown, the Vatican, and other important players at the Paris climate summit. And it was.

But we knew we had to do something different to reach a wider audience. One of the chapters in our report reviewed the state of research on climate communication, which over the past couple of decades has taught us a lot about what doesn't work. We don't know as much about what does work, but we're beginning to pull some guidelines from research. So we created a series guided by what we know to see what we could learn.

What Do We Know from the Literature?

- Facts are not enough. This is not say that facts are not important. They are. But you can try to pump as many facts as you want into people's minds and it won't necessarily change their opinions, let alone motivate action.
- Frames, narratives and values matter. People easily incorporate new facts into their existing frames (the ways they see the world), narratives (the stories they tell about

themselves and the world) and values (their beliefs about right and wrong and what matters to them). Or they can simply ignore facts that don't fit.
- Know thy audience. There are "six Americas" spread across the spectrum from alarmed to dismissive when it comes to climate change. Trying to change the minds of the dismissive is a waste of time. But the rest are potentially movable, from the concerned, to the cautious, disengaged and even doubtful. Seventy-four percent of Americans are in those middle four categories. And, yes, I include the doubtful among potentially movable audiences. Isn't science supposed to be about doubt?
- Bring people into the story of science and stimulate their curiosity. There is intriguing evidence in science communication research that invoking people's curiosity, by bringing people into the scientific process, with all of its uncertainties, can move more people to embrace science than just presenting them with the findings. This is captured in a popular meme in science communication circles: Numbers numb and stories stick.
- Messengers matter. Doctors and scientists are trusted more than journalists and politicians. Religious leaders are trusted by their flocks. People trust people who share their frames, narratives and values. This contributes to the echo chambers we tend to live in. But it's a fact of life communicators need to understand.
- Create positive instead of negative spillover. One of the cautionary findings of climate communication research is that people can easily convince themselves that they've done enough (such as recycle) and don't have to do more (such as support a carbon tax). This is a negative spillover effect. But positive spillovers happen, too, especially when people incorporate actions into their identities and think, "I'm the kind of person who drives a hybrid and believes we need to take collective action, too."

A Real-Life Experiment in Making Connections

For "Climate Lab," we wanted an approachable, even fun and humorous, trusted messenger who would appeal to diverse audiences. We found one in M. Sanjayan, the chief scientist and now CEO of Conservation International, who is also a senior researcher in the Institute of the Environment and Sustainability at UCLA. Sanjayan has lots of TV experience (PBS, BBC, National Geographic). And he was eager to try something different.

Working with the UC Office of the President's creative communications team and a professional video production crew in close collaboration with Vox, we produced six very different videos, unified by a look and feel, slick production values, great graphics, narrative arcs and Sanjayan's friendly, inviting, quizzical approach.

The subjects ranged from why people are so bad at thinking about climate change to the impacts of our consumer habits, the footprint and fate of our cellphones, food waste as a huge contributor to greenhouse gases, the past and possible future of nuclear power and the importance of diverse messengers, from the pope to a Tea Party member concerned about climate.

I recently conducted an analysis of the reception for these different stories and came away with a few conclusions that reinforce what we've learned from the literature, and give us direction for future episodes in the series.

All the stories topped half a million views and generated surprisingly on-point conversations in the comments sections. Well, mostly on-point.

But the three stories that were most popular, those that got the most views and generated the most engagement (thumbs-up and commenting), shared some important characteristics:

- The stories connected individual actions to collective actions.
- They showed agency—people taking action.
- They modeled a positive spillover effect.

These three stories were about why we need to be nudged to think about climate and like to compete to be greener than others, how we can reduce consumer waste individually and collectively, and how simple solutions can lead to big reductions in wasted food.

Two geeky, techie episodes on cellphones and nuclear energy didn't do quite as well by these measures. And though it was my favorite, the one meta story about the importance of messengers did the least well.

This tells me that people respond well to two things: stories about what they can do, and how they can be part of a broader effective change. And those two things need to be connected.

We're going to continue to experiment with "Climate Lab"—we're also creating a real online class for undergraduates which we hope will be used in other universities as well—until we get where we need to be locally and globally: carbon neutrality with a stabilizing climate by midcentury.

So, by all means, let's talk about how urgent action is, and imagine the worst results of not acting, but let's be sure to tell stories that lower the barrier to taking action, too, individually and collectively.

Periodical and Internet Sources Bibliography

The following articles have been selected to supplement the diverse views presented in this chapter.

Canadian Association of Journalists, "Media Should Cover Climate as a Crisis, Say Scientists and Journalists," Cision, November 16, 2021. https://www.newswire.ca/news-releases/media-should-cover-climate-as-a-crisis-say-scientists-and-journalists-836588074.html.

John Gibbons, "Media Must Change Its Climate Change Coverage to Help Our Planet," *Irish Examiner,* July 23, 2022. https://www.irishexaminer.com/opinion/commentanalysis/arid-40924154.html.

Mark Hertsgaard and Kyle Pope, "The Media Is Still Mostly Failing to Convey the Urgency of the Climate Crisis," the *Guardian*, June 3, 2021. https://www.theguardian.com/commentisfree/2021/jun/03/media-climate-change-crisis-emergency.

Áine Kelly-Costello, "Why Climate Change Must Stay on the News Agenda Beyond Global Summits," the Conversation, December 8, 2021. https://theconversation.com/why-climate-change-must-stay-on-the-news-agenda-beyond-global-summits-171845.

Ellen Phiddian, "Media Coverage of Climate Change Is Becoming Less Biased," *Cosmos*, August 17, 2021. https://cosmosmagazine.com/people/media-coverage-of-climate-change-is-becoming-less-biased/.

Sameera Singh, "Western Media Fails to Cover Climate Change in Most Vulnerable Countries," the Click, September 28, 2021. https://theclick.news/western-media-is-failing-to-cover-climate-change-in-the-most-vulnerable-countries/.

Raymond Snoddy, "COP27 Coverage Is a Tale of Two Media," the Media Leader, November 9, 2022. https://the-media-leader.com/snoddy-cop27-coverage-is-a-tale-of-two-media/.

Marc Tracy, "As the World Heats Up, the Climate for News Is Changing, Too," *New York Times*, July 8, 2019. https://www.nytimes.com/2019/07/08/business/media/as-the-world-heats-up-the-climate-for-news-is-changing-too.html.

Amy Westervelt and Mary Annaïse Heglar, "This Five-Point Plan Will Fix Climate Coverage," the *Nation*, October 20, 2021. https://www.thenation.com/article/environment/climate-crisis-media-coverage/.

Max Witwynski, "False Balance in News Coverage of Climate Change Makes It Harder to Address the Crisis, Northwestern Now, July 22, 2022. https://news.northwestern.edu/stories/2022/07/false-balance-reporting-climate-change-crisis/.

Kate Yoder, "Good News: The Media Is Getting the Facts Right on Climate Change," Grist, August 20, 2021. https://grist.org/science/good-news-the-media-the-facts-on-climate-change-bothsidesism/.

OPPOSING VIEWPOINTS® SERIES

CHAPTER 4

Should Climate Change Be Addressed as a Local Issue?

Chapter Preface

An oft repeated truism about American government is, "All politics is local." It seems that the politics of climate change are no exception. In the previous chapter, the viewpoints examined how the press has communicated with the public about climate change—with varying degrees of effectiveness. And for the most part, those viewpoints discussed how the national press in various countries and professional science communicators could better do their jobs. In this chapter, the authors shift their focus to examine how climate change can be addressed at the local level and by ordinary citizens. Climate change affects everyone everywhere, but talking to friends and neighbors about the local effects of climate change is the most powerful way to get the message across, according to some of the authors in this chapter.

Some experts urge us to spend less time discussing the science and more telling stories about the local impacts of climate change. Some offer tips for how to talk about climate change with family, friends, and neighbors without offending or alienating them. It's all about connection and kindness. Others question whether it is even useful to consider climate change a local issue when powerful corporations and governments are its biggest contributors.

Local means cities and towns, and those are addressed in this chapter, too. In these conversations, it is important to consider the role of cities—which are the most densely populated locales—in creating more resilient infrastructure, as well as changes to urban design that can mitigate the effects of climate change and even help reach emissions targets.

And one author here has a unique idea for conveying the urgency of the crisis to Americans. It involves math—or at least it involves expressing global temperature in a way that Americans can more easily understand and that would give American a clearer sense of just how warm things are getting.

The viewpoints in this chapter consider what it means to look for local solutions to climate change and whether these efforts are ultimately effective.

VIEWPOINT 1

> "The challenge for science communicators is . . . to make climate change feel personal, relatable and local."

We Need Powerful, Local Stories to Inspire Action on Climate Change

Kamyar Razavi

Science and science communicators have had trouble getting citizens and leaders to take climate change seriously enough to take action, Kamyar Razavi explains in this viewpoint. The solution, he says, is in storytelling. Telling stories that focus on relatable, personal experiences and create an emotional impact is key to getting people to care about climate change. These stories also have to frame climate change as a solvable problem in order for the public and leaders to become invested in it. At the time this viewpoint was published, Kamyar Razavi was a PhD candidate in the School of Communication at Simon Fraser University in British Columbia, Canada.

As you read, consider the following questions:

1. In this viewpoint, the author says that climate change does not always feel urgent. Why not?
2. According to sources cited in this viewpoint, why is sharing scientific research not enough to get leaders to take action?

"Powerful, Local Stories Can Inspire Us to Take Action on Climate Change," by Kamyar Razavi, The Conversation, September 23, 2021. https://theconversation.com/powerful-local-stories-can-inspire-us-to-take-action-on-climate-change-168177. Licensed under CC BY 4.0 International.

3. How does storytelling help people better understand the climate crisis, according to Razavi?

The climate emergency has put the world in grave peril, but that is hard to tell when watching the news or looking at the overall global response to the climate crisis, which continues to be lax.

Climate change is a complex and difficult problem to communicate. It is slow-moving, it does not always feel urgent and there is often very little gratification for acting to mitigate it.

For decades, the assumption has been that members of the public, politicians and policy makers would take the matter more seriously if only there was more information about the impacts and consequences of a warming planet.

The science, now, is unequivocal. Humans are responsible for climate change and the extreme weather events it generates.

We need to rethink the way we communicate climate change. The best tool at our disposal is a simple one: storytelling. Stories have the power to transform complex subject matters into something that feels personal, local, relatable and solvable.

But stories about the climate crisis—for example, about how people are responding in real time and making a difference—are still few and far between.

That needs to change.

The Role of Emotions

Traditionally, emotions have been seen as separate from rational judgment. Sabine Roeser, an ethics researcher, investigates the role of emotions in communicating climate change: "Emotions are generally considered to be irrational states and are hence excluded from communication and political decision making."

Emotions, Roeser argues, play a very important role in how people engage with risk. As urgent as it is, the climate crisis does not always garner the same attention as other topics, such as COVID-19 or the economy. Climate change can still feel abstract, personal and even distant.

But that is rapidly changing. Around the world, more people are starting to agree that the climate crisis is not just a distant threat, but one that will affect them personally and directly.

In Canada, concern about the personal impacts of climate change has risen seven percentage points over the past six years. In 2015, 27 percent of Canadians felt "very concerned" that the climate crisis was going to affect them personally. This past spring, that had risen to 34 percent.

This growing concern over the personal impacts of climate change represents an excellent opportunity for journalists, policy makers and environmental advocates to localize and personalize climate communication to engage people more effectively through the power of storytelling.

As important as it is to communicate information about the impacts of climate change, it is also important to include stories that people can relate to and draw inspiration from.

Improving Science Communication

Enric Sala spent years as a university professor, doing research on ocean life. He thought that his increasingly alarming reports on the state of the world's oceans would spur policy makers into action. But that did not happen so Sala left academia.

"When I was an academic, I thought that science was all we needed," he said in an interview on the podcast *Outrage and Optimism*. "That if we continued providing the scientific papers, that for some miraculous reason, leaders would read the papers."

Sala finally realized what science communicators already know: that the relationship between how much people know about the climate crisis and how they act is not necessarily linear.

"I thought that having enough information, leaders would be able to make rational decisions," Sala said. But he quickly realized that "the world doesn't work like this and most decisions are made in an irrational way."

In their book *Thinking Fast and Slow*, psychologists Daniel Kahneman and Amos Tversky famously describe the interplay

The Politics of Climate

between the "System One" brain—the intuitive, emotive, non-analytic response mechanism in our brains—and the "System Two" brain—the analytic mechanism.

As journalist Dan Gardner succinctly puts it, the challenge for science communicators is to "help System 1 feel what System 2 calculates" — to make climate change feel personal, relatable and local.

Ecological Crisis Stories

Most communication about the climate crisis builds on communicating facts and figures at people on the consequences and impacts of a warming planet.

What is missing are stories about ordinary people who are grappling with the crisis in deeply personal ways and doing

> ### Climate Change Impacts Better Addressed Through Local Wisdom
>
> Farmers' production can be maintained through the application of local wisdom and advanced technology to reduce vulnerability to the impacts of climate change, Meteorology, Climatology, and Geophysics Agency (BMKG) Chief Dwikorita Karnawati stated.
>
> "The combination of local wisdom and technology is very good. The BMKG will ensure that weather information is provided and the farmers will be able to take requisite precautionary measures," Karnawati remarked during a webinar on Village's Climate Program to build self-reliance in food production among the people living near forests held at the Brawijaya University in Malang, East Java, on Wednesday.
>
> During the pre-industrial period, there was a systemic rise in air temperature and jumped in the past three decades, thereby indicating the characteristics of air temperature change, she remarked.
>
> "That is a data-based fact. The relevant agency has also accurately measured the rising sea levels. That is also a fact," she expounded.
>
> The other fact indicating climate change pertains to extreme occurrences, including extreme drought, she pointed out.

something about it. Examples include stories of Indigenous communities fighting to protect environments from irreparable harm and students rallying for climate action.

These can be very mobilizing narratives about solutions to the climate crisis. They do not gloss over the fact that the world is in grave peril, or focus on technological quick fixes or hero worship. These stories both communicate facts and underscore the crisis the world faces.

That facts-based approach is necessary. As journalist Chris Hatch observes: "Most people still have a muddled understanding of climate breakdown—of its urgency, that it's caused overwhelmingly by fossil fuel burning, and that carbon pollution from oil, gas and coal needs to be phased out entirely."

> The BMKG chief affirmed that all occurrences are based on facts.
>
> Karnawati pointed out that in the past 15 years, the carbon dioxide (CO_2) levels rose 30 parts per million (ppm), causing the temperature and rainfall to increase frequently.
>
> The increasing number of trees felled down had eliminated the green cover that functioned as a CO_2 absorbent, she noted.
>
> Karnawati attributed farming practices, including rice cultivation at fields using fertilizers and cow manure that released methane gas, to also being contributory to greenhouse gas emissions.
>
> The BMKG chief suggested that farmers can adapt to the climate change and continue production by combining local wisdom and technology, including information and telecommunication technology as well as information and data from the BMKG, as a precautionary measure against extreme weather.
>
> "All the BMKG data has been made available to the public, including farmers, free of charge. They only need to install the BMKG info applications," she stated.
>
> Karnawati stated that tobacco farmers in Central Java have utilized rain information from the BMKG to save their tobacco plantations.
>
> "Climate change impacts better addressed through local wisdom: BMKG," ANTARA, August 20, 2020.

Fear can also play a productive role, as there is still far too much complacency. Fear can mobilize action.

But what is consistent is the power storytelling has to engage.

Effective Communication

Climate scientists—passionate about the work they do—are reacting with sadness and disbelief to the speed with which glaciers are receding in the Canadian Rockies. Coral researchers are emotionally worn out by witnessing drastic coral bleaching. And firefighters are reaching breaking points.

Stories can connect us to ecological crisis on a deeply personal level. Luckily, those personal and emotional connections are being made with increasing frequency in the news media, in documentary films and even on social media.

"I am an Incident Commander with the #BCWildfire Service," Kyle Young of the B.C. Wildfire Service tweeted during this past wildfire season. "I am writing this post rather than sharing a video message because, frankly, it would be too emotional for me."

Kyle described the physical and emotional toll the ever-intensifying wildfires in British Columbia had taken on him and his colleagues.

These stories of sacrifice and courage are among the many relatable and personalized narratives that can connect us to the climate crisis. Climate scientist Michael Mann observes that it took elementary and high school students protesting in the streets for the adults to finally take note of the urgency of the crisis.

It is no longer an abstraction. It is affecting people directly, and stories are one of the best ways to capture and communicate that urgency.

VIEWPOINT 2

> "There's a large and growing body of evidence showing that individuals can have a major impact on climate change in a number of ways."

Individual Choices Make a Difference in Fighting Climate Change

Tom Ptak

In this viewpoint, Tom Ptak asserts that even though individuals in the U.S. have a limited daily impact on energy usage, the impact of individual choices on fighting climate change is significant. This is because citizen action is a powerful source for pressuring governments and companies to take steps to increase renewable energy and cut down on emissions. According to Ptak, so far governments and geoengineering have not done enough to take action on climate. The way citizens vote and the individual consumption choices they make every day can help show politicians and companies that this should be a greater priority by making clear that constituents and consumers care about the climate. Tom Ptak is an assistant professor of geography and environmental studies at Texas State University.

"'The Average Person's Daily Choices Can Still Make a Big Difference in Fighting Climate Change—and Getting Governments and Utilities to Tackle It, Too," by Tom Ptak, The Conversation, November 22, 2021. https://theconversation.com/the-average-persons-daily-choices-can-still-make-a-big-difference-in-fighting-climate-change-and-getting-governments-and-utilities-to-tackle-it-too-170442. Licensed under CC BY 4.0 International.

The Politics of Climate

As you read, consider the following questions:

1. According to data cited in this viewpoint from the Sierra Club, how many cities, counties, and states in the U.S. had committed to transitioning to 100 percent renewable energy at the time the viewpoint was originally published?
2. According to data cited from the Natural Resources Defense Council, how many companies had promised to reduce their carbon emissions at the time this viewpoint was published?
3. What changes to transportation behaviors can help fight climate change?

The average American's everyday interactions with energy sources are limited. They range from turning appliances on or off, to commuting, to paying utility bills.

The connections between those acts and rising global temperatures may seem distant.

However, individuals hold many keys to unlocking solutions to climate change—the biggest challenge our species currently faces—which is perhaps why the fossil fuel industry spent decades misleading and misinforming the public about it.

I'm an assistant professor of geography and environmental studies at Texas State University. My research explores how geography affects the complex relationships between societies, energy and contemporary environmental challenges. I've found that the human element is critical for developing creative, effective and sustainable solutions to climate challenges.

There's a large and growing body of evidence showing that individuals can have a major impact on climate change in a number of ways. Citizen action can compel utilities to increase renewable energy and governments to enact strong climate action laws. When enough individuals make changes that lower daily household energy consumption, huge emissions reductions can result. Consumer demand can compel businesses to pursue climate and environmental sustainability.

These actions combined could bridge the "emissions gap": the significant difference between the greenhouse gas emissions expected globally and how much they need to drop in the next few decades to avoid catastrophic climate change.

Climate Change Is Outracing Government Action

People have worked for decades to slow climate change by altering national energy policies. Several states, for example, have renewable portfolio standards for utilities that require them to increase their use of renewable energy.

But 30 years of evidence from international climate talks suggests that even when nations commit on paper to reducing emissions, they seldom achieve those cuts.

The United Nations climate summits are one example. Researchers have found that many countries' pledges have been developed using flawed data.

People are also increasingly talking about geoengineering solutions for climate change. The idea is that over the coming decades, researchers will find ways to manipulate the environment to absorb more carbon pollution. However, some experts argue that geoengineering could be environmentally catastrophic. Also, there's significant doubt that technological "draw down" interventions can be perfected and scaled up soon enough to make a difference.

So if government, technology or geoengineering aren't good answers, what are?

Citizen Action

Pledges, goals and targets for shifting from fossil fuels to cleaner energy sources are only as good as the efforts by utilities and governments to reach them. Citizen participation and action have proved effective at compelling decision-makers to act. For example, scholars studying the economic, political and social dynamics that led five U.S. municipalities to adopt 100% renewable energy found that grassroots citizen advocacy was one of the key factors that drove the change.

According to the Sierra Club, through citizen-driven action, over 180 cities, more than 10 counties and eight U.S. states have made commitments to transitioning to 100% renewable energy. Consequently, over 100 million U.S residents already live in a community with a 100% renewable energy target.

Citizens have also been taking collective action at the ballot box. For example, in 2019, after New York City voters elected a more climate conscious City Council, the city enacted an ambitious emissions reduction law, and has since begun to enforce it. Also in 2019, after voters similarly shook up the state legislature, New York state enacted the Climate Leadership and Community Protection Act. Among the nation's strongest climate change laws, New York's measure mandates that the state shift to 100% renewable energy by 2040 and that its emissions from all sources drop 40% by 2040 and 85% by 2050.

Consumer Demand

How and where people spend their money can also influence corporate behavior. Companies and utilities are changing their products and production practices as consumers increasingly demand that they produce ecologically sustainable products and lower their carbon footprints. Scholars have documented that consumer boycotts negatively affect the wealth of a corporation's shareholders—which in turn can create pressure for a firm to change in response.

The Natural Resources Defense Council has reported that thanks to surging consumer awareness and demand, more than 565 companies have publicly pledged to slash their carbon emissions. Some of the world's biggest brands have responded to this pressure with claims of already being powered by 100% renewable energy, including Google and Apple.

Google put its global economic might behind climate solutions when it announced in 2019 that it would support the growth of renewable energy resources by making solar and wind energy deals worth US$2 billion.

One drawback to consumer demand-driven action is that it's often unclear how to hold these firms accountable for their promises. Recently, two impact investing experts suggested in Vox that since around 137 million Americans own stock in publicly traded companies, they could use their collective power as shareholders to make sure companies follow through.

Shifting Household Energy Behavior

A substantial body of research shows that small changes to everyday behaviors can significantly reduce energy demand. This may be the biggest way individuals and families can contribute to lowering fossil fuel consumption and reducing carbon emissions.

These steps include weatherization and using energy-efficient appliances, as well as energy efficiency measures such as turning down thermostats, washing laundry with cold water and air-drying it rather than using a dryer.

So is shifting transportation behavior. Using public transportation, car pooling, riding a bicycle or walking can significantly reduce individual and cumulative emissions.

So since most governments aren't acting quickly enough, and many technology and geoengineering solutions are still unproven or come with high risks, emission reduction goals won't be achieved without incorporating additional strategies.

The evidence is clear that these strategies should include millions of average people factoring climate change into their everyday activities regarding their communities, purchases and personal energy use.

As the environmentalist Bill McKibben wrote in 2006 about dealing with climate change, "There are no silver bullets, only silver buckshot."

VIEWPOINT 3

> "One of the most powerful things we as individuals can do to fight climate change is simple—talk to people about climate change."

Connect, Bond, and Inspire for Effective Climate Conversations

Aven Frey

In this viewpoint, Aven Frey talks with Dr. Katharine Hayhoe, a scientist and climate communicator who offers tips for successful conversations about climate change. Hayhoe is not just a scientist, but is also an evangelical Christian, a position that makes her uniquely qualified to communicate across the political divide. According to Dr. Hayhoe, finding a way to connect climate change to the things that matter most to an individual is an effective way to facilitate these conversations. Aven Frey is an outreach communications specialist for the Washington State Department of Health. At the time this viewpoint was published, she was a senior development associate for the Sightline Institute.

As you read, consider the following questions:

1. According to Dr. Hayhoe, what is one of the best things we can to do fight climate change?

"Three Steps to Better Climate Conversations," by Aven Frey, Sightline Institute, July 5, 2018. Used with permission from Sightline Institute (sightline.org).

2. Why does Dr. Hayhoe find it effective to let people know she's a Christian?
3. Why is it important to talk about solutions as well as problems?

Esteemed climate communicator Dr. Katharine Hayhoe is back on the lecture circuit with a new talk, which I was lucky enough to catch at the University of Washington in mid-May. Dr. Hayhoe's life and credentials make her uniquely suited to bridge divides and speak from the heart about climate science: She's a Canadian expat in Texas, an atmospheric scientist and political scientist at Texas Tech, and an Evangelical Christian. She's produced a trove of stellar science and messaging resources. We've shared her climate communication tips before, and her message hasn't changed: Climate change is real. It's us. It's bad. And there are all kinds of solutions.

But conversations about climate aren't always so simple.

Increasing numbers of Americans, liberal and conservative, say they are worried about climate change, but too many (including plenty of the people in charge, elected or otherwise) are in different stages of complacency or compartmentalization—or denial. Dr. Hayhoe says the best thing we can do is talk about climate change more with people we know—and in personal terms. She reminds us to start with values, not facts. Piling on more facts and data doesn't work and can even backfire. Why?

"Because when it comes to climate change," she wrote recently in Science, "science-y sounding objections are a mere smokescreen to hide the real reasons, which have much more to do with identity and ideology than data and facts."

When people feel that the policy solutions challenge their fundamental beliefs (government regulations, taxes, or restrictions on consumption), it's easier to find a way to reject the science. In fact, the best predictor of whether a person acknowledges the

The Politics of Climate

reality of human-caused global warming is their political identity, not their scientific knowledge.

Partisanship compounds other barriers. For some, there's a sense that "only a certain kind of person" cares about climate change. Numbers are growing, but many Americans aren't aware of the scientific consensus about man-made climate change (a powerful "gateway belief" that could move the needle on other climate attitudes.) For others, feeling there's nothing we can do about it can lead to apathy or paralysis. This number is growing too, but most Americans don't think climate impacts will affect them personally.

So, where to begin? According to Dr. Hayhoe, one of the most powerful things we as individuals can do to fight climate change is simple—talk to people about climate change. The truth is that most Americans rarely discuss global warming themselves and a majority say they hear little about it in the media.

Dr. Hayhoe challenges all of us to have more climate conversations. Here's her three-part formula for relevant, constructive, and hopeful climate talk.

Bond

First, says Dr. Hayhoe, find common ground. In other words, start by finding values, concerns, and experiences you share (not with a barrage of facts and figures).

"As uncomfortable as this is for a scientist in today's world," Dr. Hayhoe writes, "the most effective thing I've done is to let people know that I am a Christian. Why? Because it's essential to connect the impacts of a changing climate directly to what's already meaningful in one's life, and for many people, faith is central to who they are."

Religious or not, she reminds us that "nearly every human on the planet already has the values they need to care about climate change." She suggests finding genuine ways to connect with others—bonding over a shared love of gardening or health concerns or a shared interest in national security. Building trust helps breaks down walls built up by partisanship.

Connect

Find personal, relevant ways to show why climate matters. Dr. Hayhoe suggests connecting heart to head: talk about how climate change matters to the people and places we care about. Help people see how the science relates to your shared everyday experiences. It's not about polar bears and ice caps—it's about us, right here at home. Talk about local climate impacts and what they've meant for real people.

For example, Dr. Hayhoe knows her Texan neighbors are acutely aware of the devastating impacts of drought on their state, and since climate change is making droughts more severe, she links the science to their existing concerns. You could talk about health problems exacerbated by heat or pollution. Or maybe you both like the same Northwest brews—climate change affects beer, too!

Inspire

Demonstrate how real-life climate solutions are working. If we only talk about the daunting challenge of climate change or the difficult impacts without offering hopeful solutions, Dr. Hayhoe warns, then people's natural defense mechanism is to disassociate from the reality of the problem. To change minds and bring people aboard, we can't forget this third step: inspiring with practical, viable, and attractive solutions. People get excited about technology and efficiency. In fact, seven out of 10 Americans support prioritizing renewable energy like wind and solar, over oil, coal, and natural gas, according to an April 2018 Gallup poll. But most of us don't necessarily know about solutions working for people and communities in our neighborhood or our state. When you're talking about solutions, your conversation isn't about science anymore, but about working together to solve this problem in ways that resonate with the shared values you've established.

The Politics of Climate

For example, Dr. Hayhoe capitalizes on Texas state pride, and gets people's attention by pointing out that the state is already a leader in wind energy production, and boasting that three of the nation's top ten cities for solar power potential are in Texas. Dr. Hayhoe knows people in her neighborhood not only admire her efficient plug-in electric car once they know how much money she saves on gas, but love the idea of taking advantage of Texas' vast wealth of renewable energy potential to save Texas families money on energy bills and taxes, and to create local jobs, and help to ease the devastating droughts made longer and more severe by a changing climate.

These three steps make for easier, more powerful climate conversations. And Dr. Hayhoe challenges us all to go out and have those conversations!

VIEWPOINT 4

> "Discussing global warming . . . in Fahrenheit converts abstract scientific measurements into actual lived experiences."

When Talking About Climate Change, Speak Like the Locals

Jason Mark

As Jason Mark explains in this viewpoint, sometimes whether communication works or not comes down to seemingly small things. In this viewpoint, the author suggests a simple change in terminology that could make a huge difference in conveying the danger and urgency of climate change: by talking about the impacts of climate change in degrees Fahrenheit instead of Celsius for the American public. Making this small change to the language used would help Americans better understand the issue and its impacts. There are also other small changes in rhetoric that can help engage communities. Jason Mark is a writer and editor for Sierra, the magazine of the Sierra Club.

As you read, consider the following questions:

1. What does Mark mean by "situational rhetoric"?
2. Why do most discussions of global warming use the Celsius scale?

"Fahrenheit > Celsius," by Jason Mark, Sierra Club, June 3, 2019. Reprinted by permission. This article was originally published in Sierra Magazine.

3. Why would speaking about rising temperatures in Fahrenheit rather than Celsius be more "visceral," according to this viewpoint?

For the better part of 20 years, environmental policy wonks, activists, journalists, and academics have debated, sometimes acrimoniously, how best to communicate the existential danger of dismantling Earth's once stable climate. Should we frame climate change as a hopeful opportunity to address other social ills, or are we best served speaking in fearsome language about how truly awful the changes to Earth could be? Maybe climate change should be couched in the language of past accomplishments—the wartime mobilization of World War II or the inspiring activism of the women's suffrage and civil rights movements. Or maybe we should dwell on the dangers of the problem. Perhaps it's just a matter of using stronger language; in May, *The Guardian* released a new style guide for its writers that encouraged using more urgent terms like "climate crisis" and "global heating."

While I've got some opinions of my own, I mostly lean toward an all-of-the-above strategy: Use whatever global warming/global heating, climate change/climate crisis language you think will work best, depending upon whom you're talking to. Call it "situational rhetoric."

I do, however, have one modest proposal to make. We should stop talking about rising global temperatures in Celsius and use the measurement that Americans understand best: the Fahrenheit scale.

Since the vast majority of the world measures temperatures in Celsius, and since Celsius is the default measurement for scientists, most climate change communication takes place using the 1-to-100 scale. But for the 325 million people in the United States, Cclsius is the equivalent of Latin. It means nothing to Americans.

A quick Google search reveals the challenge of talking about climate change in Celsius. Imagine a climate science neophyte who wants to better understand the goals outlined in the Paris

Agreement and who types "1.5 degrees Celsius in Fahrenheit" into the search engine. Here's what they'd get:

Thirty-four degrees? Sounds cold. Even worse, seems confusing.

For most Americans, the metric system, and the Celsius scale in particular, is baffling. (I mean, why is a kilogram greater than a pound but a kilometer is shorter than a mile?) Temperature measurements in Celsius are meaningless. A 40°C day in Barcelona is sweltering; a 40°F day in Baltimore is frigid.

The problem with discussing climate change in Celsius is that it understates the scale and intensity of the climate threat. A 1.5° or 2°C increase in average global temperatures simply doesn't sound like much to Americans.

Imagine if we were to consistently talk about climate change in Fahrenheit. One degree of Celsius is the equivalent to 1.8 degrees Fahrenheit. Do the math: 1.5°C becomes a 2.7°F rise in average global temperatures; a 2°C rise is the equivalent of a 3.6°F rise.

I suspect (and I admit this is little more than supposition) that numbers like 2.7 and 3.6 will still sound modest to many people. But I think the situation changes as the conversation turns to the most worrisome climate change scenarios.

Even if every country meets it obligations under the Paris Agreement, we're on track to hit 3°C of global warming by the end of the century, according to the number crunchers at Climate Action Tracker. Now we're talking about 5.4°F—the difference between a lovely spring day and a warm one. In the absence of meaningful action—a terrifying though realistic scenario given that greenhouse gas emissions continue to rise—we could be on track for as much as 4.4°C of warming by 2100. That's nearly 8°F—the difference between a warm day and an uncomfortably hot one. Eight degrees is the spread between the average August high temperature in Kansas City and the average August high temperature in Minneapolis, more than 400 miles to the north. It's a big deal.

In short, to talk about global warming in Fahrenheit doesn't just make the climate conversation more intelligible to more people.

It makes the conversation visceral. Discussing global warming—or global heating, if you prefer—in Fahrenheit converts abstract scientific measurements into actual lived experiences. Fahrenheit is how Americans know the weather, how they feel it on their skin. If we want people to really get the direness of the climate crisis, we need to hit them where they feel, not simply where they think.

Some climate communicators are already doing this. The good folks at InsideClimate News and Vox often (though not always) give readers figures in both Celsius and Fahrenheit. The only problem is that usually the more colloquial measurement of Fahrenheit is relegated to a parenthetical. The presumptions of understanding are backward. Fahrenheit should come first in order to connect with the greatest number of readers, and then Celsius second, to satisfy the science nerds and wonks among us.

So, all you journalists and activists and public-facing scientists, let's get together and keep in mind this simple formula for mainstream climate change communication: $F > C$. It's a small thing, but who knows—it might just have a large impact. If we can do a little bit better at speaking in plain English measurements, we've got a better chance at avoiding those worst-case scenarios.

VIEWPOINT 5

> "Well designed, compact, walkable cities with good public transport greatly reduce our per capita carbon footprint."

Cities Are Both a Cause of and Solution to Climate Change

United Nations

In this viewpoint, the United Nations' UN News interviews UN-Habitat Executive Director Maimunah Mohd Sharif. The topic is cities. Cities are both a primary contributor to climate change and the most affected by climate change. However, according to Sharif, they may also be a key part of the solution. By focusing on what cities can do to help address the effects of climate change, local actions have the potential to make a big difference. In addition to her role at the UN, Sharif is a Malaysian politician and urban planner. The United Nations (UN) is an intergovernmental organization with the goal of promoting international cooperation on key issues, including climate change.

As you read, consider the following questions:

1. What changes in urban design would help mitigate global warming, according to Sharif?

From "Cities: A Cause of and Solution to' Climate Change" ©2019 United Nations. Reprinted with the permission of the United Nations. https://news.un.org/en/story/2019/09/1046662

2. What can cities to do prepare for the already unavoidable impacts of climate change?
3. Why are the poor hit harder by the effects of climate change, according to Sharif?

Cities around the world are the "main cause of climate change" but can also offer a part of the solution to reducing the harmful greenhouses gases that are causing global temperatures to rise according to UN-Habitat Executive Director Maimunah Mohd Sharif.

Ms. Sharif will be joining world leaders at United Nations headquarters in New York next week at the Climate Action Summit convened by the UN Secretary-General António Guterres.

UN-Habitat is supporting one of the nine action tracks designated by the Secretary-General "Infrastructure, Cities and Local Action" under the leadership of the Governments of Kenya and Turkey.

UN News asked the UN-Habitat Executive Director what role cities should play in slowing down climate change.

Q: Why are cities an important part of tackling climate change?

A: Over half of the world's population lives in cities, and this is likely to increase to over two-thirds by 2030. Cities use a large proportion of the world's energy supply and are responsible for around 70 percent of global energy-related greenhouse gas emissions which trap heat and result in the warming of Earth.

Levels of carbon dioxide, the most prevalent greenhouse gas, are at the highest levels ever, mostly due to the burning of fossil fuels for energy.

The huge carbon footprint created by our cities results from poor planning and layout. Low-density suburban sprawl with little public transport and homes far from work and shops means more cars on the roads emitting carbon dioxide. In addition, most of the ever-increasing number of buildings still use fossil fuels for their energy needs.

Cities, while being the main cause of climate change, are also the most affected. Most cities are situated near water putting them at risk from rising sea levels and storms. However, given their role as hubs of innovation and creativity, we also look to cities to provide us with answers. Energy, building, mobility and planning solutions and innovations in cities have the potential to deliver major emission cuts.

Q: How can cities contribute to reducing climate change?

A: Huge gains, in terms of reducing harmful gases, can be made by changing how we plan, build, manage and power our cities and towns. Well designed, compact, walkable cities with good public transport greatly reduce our per capita carbon footprint and are key to achieving many of the Sustainable Development Goals of which climate action is a key part.

We urgently need to reduce the amount of carbon dioxide produced by our homes and offices by moving to zero carbon buildings, which do not use any carbon for heating, lighting, cooling or electricity. They can manage this by becoming more energy efficient and using renewable energy sources.

Our expanding cities, towns and villages can create buildings and infrastructure that are highly energy efficient and designed with the local climate in mind using innovative technologies. For example, most of the new buildings in the next 30 years will be in Africa and Asia which should move away from air conditioning and maximize natural ventilation.

To power our cities we must generate clean, resource-efficient energy and move away from fossil fuels. Since 2009, the cost of renewable electricity has dropped both for solar and wind power and will keep going down as more of us use them.

The extraction and manufacturing of materials for buildings such as steel and concrete and construction processes produce carbon dioxide so using low carbon infrastructure will also slash emissions.

Transport also produces significant amounts of emissions. Cities need should not be planned around cars but people and should invest in zero-carbon public transport, footpaths and protected bike lanes. Electric public transport, powered through renewable energy could prevent 250 million tonnes of carbon emissions by 2030, as well as improving people's health, and lowering noise and air pollution in our cities.

Organic matter emits methane as it decomposes, which is a much more powerful greenhouse gas than carbon dioxide in the short-term, so it's key to minimize organic waste by improving waste management methods and to take steps to capture and use the methane emissions from landfills.

And in addition to the long-term solutions that require a change in the way our economies operate, we can all make personal choices to alter our lifestyle and consumption patterns.

Q: Climate change is already happening and affecting cities, how can cities prepare for this new reality?

A: The effects of the recent changes in the planet's climate, as well as expected future climate risks have pushed about a thousand cities worldwide to declare a climate emergency.

Climate adaptation, whereby cities adjust to actual or expected future climate, is a sound investment. This can include early warning systems, climate-resilient infrastructure and housing, and investments in water resources. The 2019 Global Commission on Adaptation Report shows that investing US$1.8 trillion in climate adaptation can generate US$7.1 trillion in total benefits.

Resilient shelter will only work if we have resilient communities. I have recently met the Commonwealth Secretary-General, Patricia Scotland, and other world leaders and we are committed to working together to ensure we build back better. Our focus on "Infrastructure, Cities and Local Action" is part of the larger UN-Habitat Strategic Plan to build climate resilience worldwide."

Q: To what extent are the poorest and most vulnerable people most impacted by climate change in cities?

A: The least well off in our cities and communities will bear the brunt of climate change in the form of floods, landslides and extreme heat. This is because they often live in inadequate housing in fragile locations like mountain sides or floodplains, with no risk-reducing infrastructure such as functioning storm drains. Globally, there are an estimated 880 million people living in informal settlements that are highly vulnerable to climate change.

We are urging governments to plan better and build back better.

Q: How different are the challenges faced by cities in developing countries compared to those in the developed world?

A: The whole world is threatened by climate change but developing countries are often hit the hardest. They often do not have the capacity to face extreme weather events and have insufficient governance frameworks to manage climate challenges. Cities in developing countries also face barriers in accessing climate finance including a lack of focus on cities as a strategic priority. Ultimately climate change does not respect borders—everyone will all be affected and we all need to act together to stop it now.

VIEWPOINT 6

> "This polarization is allowing online discussions about climate change to be overridden by culturally-focused arguments about things like diet. This appears to be further cementing the idea that climate change is a matter of ideology, making it harder to convince people to support action to tackle it."

Reducing Climate Action to Individual Choices Has a Harmful Effect

Taha Yasseri and Mary Sanford

In this viewpoint, Taha Yasseri and Mary Sanford explain how the tendency to reduce conversations to personal, culturally focused arguments on social media makes the conversation around climate change more polarized and reduces it to a culture war, which has a detrimental effect on encouraging individuals to rally around the cause. The authors consider social media debates around veganism as an example of these harmful effects. Incendiary and polarized online discourse causes people to be repelled from those with different views and creates echo chambers. The polarization of the climate change debate that results from its focus on culturally sensitive issues like diet and cuisine weakens politicians' abilities to take action on climate change.

"Social Media Is Reducing Climate Change Debates to Your Views on Veganism," by Taha Yasseri and Mary Sanford, The Conversation, October 1, 2021. https://theconversation.com/social-media-is-reducing-climate-change-debates-to-your-views-on-veganism-167931. Licensed under CC BY 4.0 International.

Should Climate Change Be Addressed as a Local Issue?

Taha Yasseri is an associate professor at the School of Sociology and a Geary Fellow at the Geary Institute for Public Policy at University College Dublin, Ireland. At the time this viewpoint was published, Mary Sanford was a PhD candidate in social data science at the University of Oxford.

As you read, consider the following questions:

1. What example do the authors provide of how conversations about dietary choices and climate change can become polarized on social media?
2. According to the authors, what percent of the tweets they analyzed that were tagged "#veganuary" were polarized in nature, either in support of or against veganism?
3. Why do the authors say that having diet and cooking at the center of the climate culture war could be catastrophic?

Ten years ago, when we ranked the most controversial articles on Wikipedia, George W. Bush was at the top of the list with global warming at number five. The article on global warming has now been re-titled as climate change, but this remains among the most polarizing issues of our time—and one frequently debated on social media.

This might seem like it's due to the way climate change is often presented primarily as a political issue: something you can choose whether or not to support. But perhaps it's as much a result of the way social media works. Our recent research shows that polarization on social media is mathematically inevitable.

What's more, this polarization is allowing online discussions about climate change to be overridden by culturally-focused arguments about things like diet. This appears to be further cementing the idea that climate change is a matter of ideology, making it harder to convince people to support action to tackle it.

The fact that it's so easy to unfriend or unfollow people you disagree with on social media has accelerated the formation of online echo chambers to the extent that even an algorithmic tool designed to break the bubbles won't be able to help.

Don't get us wrong: we're big fans of social media and most likely have already tweeted this article by the time you read it. Social media can be seen as a marketplace of ideas, providing an open forum to exchange facts and opinions and, importantly for scientists, to inform the public about their research. But polarization can ruin it for everyone.

An example of this relates to the UK bakery chain Greggs' vegan sausage roll, which ignited days of social media turmoil when it was introduced to the U.K. in January 2019 to coincide with Veganuary, a month-long U.K.-based charity campaign designed to encourage veganism. Veganuary-oriented social media discussions that year were dominated by arguments over the sausage roll's relative merits.

To understand the extent of this interference, we analyzed about half a million tweets posted between 28 December 2018 and 28 January 2019 containing any of the hashtags "#vegan", "#veganuary" and "#veganuary2019" to map out the prevalence of extreme opinions among the tweets.

Around 30% of the tweets we analyzed were firmly pro-vegan, while 20% of tweets used Veganuary-related hashtags to express their protest against veganism. More importantly, many Twitter users who tweeted about Veganuary explicitly said if it wasn't for the Greggs story, they wouldn't have gotten involved.

On one hand, bringing extra attention to the campaign might be considered a blessing. On the other, the polarized nature of online arguments disproportionately focused on the issue of the vegan sausage roll.

This shifted what could have been a fruitful and logical discussion around the pros and cons of veganism towards unproductive fights centred around perceived threats to people's identities tied up with what they do or don't eat and what that means. Many quickly took sides, refusing to engage in conversation and instead attacking the personal qualities or intelligence of the "other side."

This conflict surfaced again on social media a few months later, when the Intergovernmental Panel on Climate Change (IPCC), a U.N.-endorsed organization, published its Special Report on Climate Change and Land in August 2019. In order to gauge the level of public engagement with the report, we collected all tweets sent in August 2019 which contained the phrase "IPCC." We then used software to analyze the content of some 6,000 tweets in English in order to extract the main topics of discussion.

We found that not only were a large portion of the tweets in response to the IPCC report specifically about diet, but these tweets contained the most toxic and polarized language in the sample. This is even more surprising when considering that diet was only mentioned briefly in the original IPCC report, without any explicit recommendations about meat or dairy consumption.

Evidence like this suggests that diet and cooking are now forming the core of a new culture war around climate.

This could be catastrophic for climate action. Politicians and policy makers traditionally tend to avoid issues that are culturally controversial, and polarization of public opinion has been shown to weaken politicians' accountability when it comes to making major decisions.

Our work recently published in Climatic Change shows how tools such as computational topic modelling and sentiment analysis can be used to monitor public discourse about topics like climate events, diet and climate policies. This could help policymakers plan more engaging communication strategies: in other words, to help them read the room.

Both scientists and science communicators who discuss reports like that produced by the IPCC must understand, and anticipate, the likelihood of emotionally charged, potentially negative responses to such polarizing issues as climate change—as well as specific areas of polarization, such as diet, that are currently more popular. This way, they can work to communicate key information in ways that allow readers to focus on what really matters.

Periodical and Internet Sources Bibliography

The following articles have been selected to supplement the diverse views presented in this chapter.

Maggie Astor, "As Federal Climate-Fighting Tools Are Taken Away, Cities and States Step Up," *New York Times*, July 1, 2022. https://www.nytimes.com/2022/07/01/climate/climate-policies-cities-states-local.html.

Jillian Blanchard, "Local Governments Can Use Their Power to Combat Climate Change," *Bloomberg Law*, June 3, 2021. https://news.bloomberglaw.com/environment-and-energy/local-governments-can-use-their-power-to-combat-climate-change-17.

Jessica Brown, "How Cities Are Going Carbon Neutral," BBC, November 16, 2021. https://www.bbc.com/future/article/20211115-how-cities-are-going-carbon-neutral.

Jill Dvorkin, "Climate Change: What Can Local Governments Do?" MRSC, October 8, 2020. https://mrsc.org/stay-informed/mrsc-insight/october-2020/climate-change-what-can-local-governments-do.

Aitor Hernández-Morales, "UN Report: Rethink Cities to Combat Climate Crisis," *Politico*, April 4, 2022. https://www.politico.eu/article/city-rethink-need-combat-climate-crisis-ipcc/.

Joe McCarthy, "Eight Ways Cities Are Healing the Planet," Global Citizen, April 21, 2022. https://www.globalcitizen.org/en/content/how-cities-are-protecting-the-environment/.

Huw Oliver, Ed Cunningham, and Sophie Dickinson, "21 Amazing Things Cities Are Doing to Fight the Climate Crisis," Time Out, November 10, 2021. https://www.timeout.com/things-to-do/cities-leading-the-fight-against-climate-change.

Deepa Padmanaban, "How Cities Can Fight Climate Change," *Knowable*, June 9, 2022. https://knowablemagazine.org/article/food-environment/2022/how-cities-can-fight-climate-change.

Sam Ricketts, Rita Cliffton, Lola Oduyeru, and Bill Holland, "States Are Laying a Roadmap for Climate Leadership," Center for American Progress, April 30, 2020. https://www.americanprogress.org/article/states-laying-road-map-climate-leadership/.

Joshua A. Schwartz and Sabrina B. Arias, "Americans Agree with Their State and Local Officials on Climate Action," *Washington Post*, July 26, 2022. https://www.washingtonpost.com/politics/2022/07/26/local-climate-california-net-zero/.

Laurie Winkless, "Rethinking Our Cities to Tackle Climate Change," *Forbes*, April 21, 2022. https://www.forbes.com/sites/lauriewinkless/2022/04/21/rethinking-our-cities-to-tackle-climate-change/?sh=4ad2d5175766.

For Further Discussion

Chapter 1

1. In this chapter, we saw how climate change has become politicized, with many people seeing it as a part of a "leftwing agenda." How did an issue that affects everyone on the planet and was once non-partisan come to be seen as an issue for one particular party or political agenda? Can you think of other issues that have morphed in this way?
2. Why would powerful economic interests (such as large corporations) be troubled by international accords to address climate change? What have these interests done to block climate action?
3. Some of the viewpoints in this chapter discuss the 2022 Inflation Relief Act (IRA), which is the first major piece of climate legislation Congress has passed in decades. Based on what you have read, do you think it does enough to address climate change? Explain your answer.

Chapter 2

1. Based on the viewpoints in this chapter, what disadvantages do poorer, developing nations face in addressing the effects of climate change? What could be done to help with this?
2. In the viewpoint by Jacqueline Peel and Zoe Nay, the authors mention that the United Nations (UN) has requested an advisory opinion from the International Court of Justice (ICJ) on countries' obligations for climate change. Do you think there should be international laws in place making these obligations more concrete?

For Further Discussion

Why or why not? If so, what do you think having laws would change?
3. In the viewpoint by John Vogler and Marit Hammond, the authors argue that shifting the focus of climate justice from countries to individuals would make it more effective? Do you agree with this argument? Why or why not?

Chapter 3

1. In your experience, has the media done a good job of covering the issue of climate change and educating the public about the science behind? What examples can you give to support your view?
2. The viewpoint by Stephan Lewandowsky and Michael Ashley in this chapter focuses on the Australian media. Do you think that media in the United States and Canada are guilty of some of the same mistakes? What examples can you give?
3. In the viewpoint by Denise-Marie Ordway, the author claims that making small changes to the type of language used by the media in content about climate change would make a big difference in engaging the public's attention and making the discussion less polarized. What examples does the author give of ways the media could do this? Do you think this would be effective? Why or why not?

Chapter 4

1. The science of climate change has been convincing for many years, but only recently have the effects been felt by people in their communities. Do you think stories of floods, storms, droughts, and other extreme weather, told by people who are living through these crises have contributed to the increase in public concern about climate change?

2. The viewpoint by Aven Frey offers tips about how to talk to others about climate change. Have you had conversations about climate change with friends, family, or neighbors? How did it go? What have you learned about what works and what doesn't work when trying to connect with people about this issue?
3. This final chapter has been about climate change as a local issue. Has your community experienced any of the effects of climate change? Has it implemented any plans to either reduce carbon emissions or mitigate the effects of climate change?

Organizations to Contact

The editors have compiled the following list of organizations concerned with the issues debated in this book. The descriptions are derived from materials provided by the organizations. All have publications or information available for interested readers. The list was compiled on the date of publication of the present volume; the information provided here may change. Be aware that many organizations take several weeks or longer to respond to inquiries, so allow as much time as possible.

350.org
20 Jay Street
Suite 732
Brooklyn, NY 11201
email: Natalia@350.org
website: https://350.org

350.org is a non-profit organization building a global climate movement through grassroots organizing and mass public actions. Its website includes information for finding local groups to join.

Action for Climate Emergency (ACE)
529 Main Street
Suite 200
Charlestown, MA 02129
(617) 274-8835
email: hello@acespace.org
website: https://acespace.org

Action for Climate Emergency is an organization that educates students about climate change and empowers them to lead on climate solutions. It encourages young people to lead the global climate movement and make the movement more just and equitable.

The Climate Reality Project

555 11th Street NW
Suite 601
Washington, DC 20004
website: www.climaterealityproject.org

The Climate Reality Project is a nonprofit organization that recruits, trains, and mobilizes people to take climate action. It aims to create a more diverse, inclusive, and equitable climate movement.

Corporate Accountability

10 Milk Street, Suite 610
Boston, MA 02108
(617) 695-2525
website: https://corporateaccountability.org

This organization works to stop transnational organizations from devastating democracy, the environment, and human rights and create a world where corporations answer to people, not the other way around. The company uses strategic campaigns that compels transnational corporations to focus more on the environment and human rights and governments to stop doing their bidding.

David Suzuki Foundation

219-2211 West 4th Ave.
Vancouver, BC V6K 4S2
(604) 732-4228
website: www.davidsuzuki.org

Founded in 1990, the David Suzuki Foundation is a national, bilingual nonprofit organization headquartered in Vancouver, with offices in Toronto and Montreal. The foundation uses science, education, and advocacy to promote solutions that conserve nature and help achieve sustainability. Through evidence-based research, education, and policy analysis, the foundation works to conserve and protect the natural environment and help create a sustainable Canada.

Extinction Rebellion

website: https://rebellion.global

Extinction Rebellion is an international, decentralized, nonpartisan movement. Members use non-violent actions and civil disobedience to pressure to act with justice on climate and environmental issues.

Green America

1612 K Street NW, Suite 1000
Washington, DC 20006
(800) 584-7336
website: https://greenamerica.org

Green America uses the economic power of consumers, investors, businesses, and the marketplace to help create a more socially just and environmentally sustainable society. The organization helps educate and mobilize consumers and support green businesses.

Natural Resources Defense Council (NRDC)

40 West 20th Street
11th Floor
New York, NY 10011
(212) 727-2700
email: nrdcinfo@nrdc.org
website: www.nrdc.org

This grassroots environmental organization helps promote green living and finds other ways to protect the environment. Its website publishes articles by scientists and other environmental experts that educate and encourage both individual effort and community-based activism.

Union of Concerned Scientists

Two Brattle Square
Cambridge, MA 02138-3780
(617) 547-5552
website: www.ucsusa.org

The Politics of Climate

The Union of Concerned Scientists is a nonprofit science advocacy organization based in the U.S. whose members include private citizens and professional scientists. Its mission is to use rigorous science to solve the planet's most pressing problems, including addressing the threats posed by climate change.

Zero Hour

820 Ritchie Hwy Unit 250
Sevema Park, MD 21146
email: info@thisiszerohour.org
website: www.thisiszerohour.org

Zero Hour is a youth-led movement offering training and resources for a new generation of climate-change activists who want to take concrete action about climate change. Their goal is to protect the rights of the next generation to a clean, safe, and healthy environment.

Bibliography of Books

Rachel Carson. *Silent Spring and other Writings on the Environment.* New York, NY: Library of America, 2018.

Jessica Fanzo. *Can Fixing Dinner Fix the Planet?* Baltimore, MD: Johns Hopkins University Press, 2021.

John Freeman, ed. *Tales of Two Planets: Stories of Climate Change and Inequality in a Divided World.* New York, NY: Penguin, 2020.

Bill Gates. *How to Avoid a Climate Disaster: The Solutions We Have and the Breakthroughs We Need.* New York, NY: Knopf, 2021.

Dina Gilio-Whitaker. *As Long as Grass Grows: The Indigenous Fight for Environmental Justice, from Colonization to Standing Rock.* Boston, MA: Beacon Press, 2020.

Katharine Hayhoe. *Saving Us: A Climate Scientist's Case for Hope and Healing in a Divided World.* New York, NY: One Signal, 2021.

Bridey Heing and Erica Grove, eds. *Sustainable Consumption* (Current Controversies). New York, NY: Greenhaven Publishing, 2021.

Avery Elizabeth Hurt. *A Global Threat: The Emergence of Climate Change Science* (History of Conservation: Preserving Our Planet). New York, NY: Cavendish Square, 2018.

Avery Elizabeth Hurt. *Key Environmental Laws* (Laws That Changed History). New York, NY: Cavendish Square, 2020.

Hope Jahren. *The Story of More: How We Got to Climate Change and Where We Go from Here.* New York, NY: Penguin, 2020.

Ayana Elizabeth Johnson and Katharine K. Wilkinson, eds. *All We Can Save: Truth, Courage, and Solutions for the Climate Crisis*. New York, NY: One World, 2021.

Naomi Klein. *This Changes Everything: Capitalism Versus the Climate*. New York, NY: Simon and Schuster, 2014.

Elizabeth Kolbert. *Field Notes from a Catastrophe: Man, Nature, and Climate Change*. New York, NY: Bloomsbury, 2015.

Naomi Oreskes and Erik M. Conway. *Merchants of Doubt: How a Handful of Scientists Obscured the Truth on Issues from Tobacco Smoke to Global Warming*. New York, NY: Bloomsbury, 2010.

Nathaniel Rich. *Losing Earth: A Recent History*. New York, NY: Farrar, Straus and Giroux, 2019.

Greta Thunberg. *The Climate Book: The Facts and the Solutions*. New York, NY: Penguin, 2023.

Robin Wall Kimmerer. *Braiding Sweetgrass: Indigenous Wisdom, Scientific Knowledge, and the Teachings of Plants*. Minneapolis, MN: Milkweed Editions, 2015.

Index

A

activism, 90, 138, 150
advertising, 111–112, 114, 122
agriculture, 25, 28, 63–65, 69, 76, 136–137, 147
Arrhenius, Svente, 92–93
Ashcroft, Linden, 91–96
Ashley, Michael, 97–103

B

Babin, Madeline, 24–28
balance in media, 90–91, 98, 101–102, 108
Bernards, Nick, 36–40
Bhandary, Rishikesh Ram, 68–72
Biddlestone, Mikey, 104–108
Biden, Joe, 14, 19–20, 24–25, 27, 42–43, 59
Brown, Jerry, 124–125

C

Camara, Isatou, 64–65
carbon credit, 37–38
carbon tax, 20–21, 49, 51, 77–81, 126
Center for Biological Diversity, 27
Christensen, Jon, 123–128
Clean Development Mechanism, 37–38
Climate Change Performance Index, 19–20

climate denial/skepticism, 14–15, 52, 90, 91, 94–103, 109–110, 113–114, 116–122
climate disaster/weather, 15, 27, 53, 62, 68, 73, 121, 134, 137
   drought, 26, 48, 63, 119, 136, 147–148
   extreme temperatures, 63, 65, 69, 93, 96, 105–106, 110, 119, 132, 140, 147, 151, 154, 157
   flooding, 48, 63, 69, 74, 76, 105, 119, 157
   hurricane/typhoon/cyclone, 26, 51, 63–65, 74–76, 84
   wildfire, 26, 138
climate/environmental justice, 15, 25, 50, 52, 54, 64, 73–74, 76, 84
climate equity, 50–52, 54
climate finance, 15, 26, 48–86
climate investment, 20, 24–25, 27–28
climate migration/refugees, 51, 53, 63–64
Clinton, Bill, 20–21
Coleman, Renita, 116–119, 121–122
Congress (U.S.), 15, 18–26, 28, 41–44, 59, 80, 95, 114
   Senate, 20, 23, 78
corporations, 18, 22–23, 30–31, 36–41, 44, 49, 51–52, 79, 81, 107, 110–111, 139–140, 142
Cunningham, Richard, 19–23

D

deforestation, 39, 99
democracy, 20, 29–35, 115
Democratic Party, 22–23, 43, 81, 114, 119
developing countries, 50–51, 56–76, 157
diet, 158–161

E

economy, 15, 18, 51, 53, 60, 78, 80–81, 134, 141
ecosystem, 22, 54–55
electric vehicles, 21, 25–26, 39, 44, 93, 148, 156
emissions, 14, 21, 25, 27–28, 31, 36–39, 49–53, 56–57, 59–60, 63, 65–66, 74–75, 80–81, 84, 99, 106, 124, 132, 137, 140–143, 151, 154–156
energy efficiency, 25, 44, 143, 155–156
Environmental Protection Agency (EPA), 28, 41–44
ethics, 15, 49–50, 53–55, 61, 76, 90, 118, 134
European Court of Human Rights, 85
executive order, 24, 28
extinction, 63, 106

F

food insecurity, 53
fossil fuel, 21–22, 37, 29, 50–51, 60, 66–67, 77, 91–96, 107, 109–111, 115, 124, 140–141, 143, 155
coal, 41–42, 44, 59, 70, 78–80, 92–93, 137, 147
gasoline, 78, 112–113, 137, 148
natural gas, 26–27, 112, 147
oil, 27, 74, 78–79, 93–94, 112–113, 137, 147
Frey, Aven, 144–148

G

Gerrard, Michael, 41–44
Global Methane Pledge, 26
global warming, 14, 37, 48, 50–52, 54, 63, 75–76, 90, 93–95, 104, 116–117, 119, 121, 134, 136, 146, 152, 159
Green Climate Fund (GCF), 70–71, 75
greenhouse effect, 25, 43–44, 50, 52, 57, 66, 72, 74, 81, 91–94, 96, 120, 127, 137, 151, 154, 156
Guy, Brendan, 57, 60–61

H

Hammond, Marit, 73–76
Hansen, James, 95–96
Hayhoe, Katharine, 144–148
health, 53, 147
Hill, Alice C., 24–28
Holdren, John, 120–121

I

incentive, 18, 21, 25, 27, 39, 44, 75
Independents, 119
Indigenous communities, 137
industrialized countries, 54, 56–76

Index

Industrial Revolution, 63, 92
infrastructure, 132, 153–157
Interior Department (U.S.), 27
International Court of Justice, 82–86
International Geophysical Year, 94

J

Jimenez, Cinthia, 118, 121
jobs, 77, 79–80, 148

K

Kahneman, Daniel, 135–136
Karnawati, Dwikorita, 136–137
Kerry, John, 28
Krznaric, Roman, 29–35
Kyoto Protocol, 38, 96

L

legislation/policy, 14, 140–141
   Build Back Better Act, 20, 23
   Clean Air Act, 42–43
   Clean Power Plan (CPP), 41–42
   Climate Leadership and Community Protection Act (New York), 142
   Inflation Reduction Act (IRA), 15, 18–29, 43–44
Lewandowsky, Stephan, 97–103
Lindwall, Courtney, 56–61
lobbying, 18, 31
local solutions, 15, 132–157
Lynn, William S., 49–55

M

Macron, Emmanuel, 78
Manchin, Joe, 20
marginalized communities, 48–86, 154, 157
Mark, Jason, 149–152
McCain, John, 14–15
media, 15–16, 89–128, 132, 135, 138, 150
Metcalf, Gilbert E., 77–81
mineral extraction, 37, 39–40
misinformation, 90, 94–95, 97, 104–115, 140
Modi, Narendra, 50–51
Montreal Protocol, 95
Mottley, Mia, 63, 66

N

Napolitano, Janet, 125
National Oceanic and Atmospheric Administration (NOAA), 26
Natural Resources Defense Council (NRDC), 56–57, 60, 140, 142
Nay, Zoe, 82–86

O

oceans, 135, 138
Obama, Barack, 20, 42, 78, 114
Ordway, Denise-Marie, 116–122
Organization for Economic Cooperation and Development (OECD), 58
Osaka, Shannon, 19–24
Oxfam, 52–53, 58–59

P

Paris Agreement, 21, 74–75, 85, 150–151
Parliament (UK), 33
Peel, Jacqueline, 82–86
polarization, 16, 20, 22, 94, 111, 114, 158–161
pollution, 39–40, 42, 44, 51–52, 60, 78–81, 111, 137, 141, 147
Ptak, Tom, 139–143

R

Razavi, Kamyar, 133–138
Rees, Martin, 32–33
renewable energy, 20, 33, 36, 41–44, 60, 65, 70, 77, 110–113, 115, 139–142, 156
  solar, 21, 25, 39, 59, 78, 80, 143, 147–148, 155
  wind, 21, 26–27, 38–39, 78, 143, 147–148, 155
Republican Party, 14, 22, 43, 78, 81, 114, 119

S

Sabin Center for Climate Change Law, 44, 65
Sanford, Mary, 158–161
science, 14, 22, 90–94, 96, 98–103, 105, 107–108, 110, 113–114, 117, 120, 124, 126, 132–136, 138, 144–147, 150, 152, 160–161
Scott, Amy, 19–24
sea levels, 48, 51, 59, 64–65, 69, 106, 119, 155
Sharif, Maimunah Mohd, 153–157
Sierra Club, 140, 142
social media, 90, 94–95, 106–107, 109–115, 138, 158–16Twitter, 113–114, 159–161
Sommer, Lauren, 62–68
Stockholm Environment Institute, 52–53
Supreme Court (U.S.)
  Massachusetts v. EPA, 43
  West Virginia v. EPA, 28, 41, 43–44

T

technology, 25, 39, 80, 93, 137, 141, 147, 155
Thorson, Esther, 118, 121
Thunberg, Greta, 41
Tigre, Maria Antonia, 65–66
Trump, Donald, 42, 78, 115
Turrentine, Jeff, 109–115
Tversky, Amos, 135–136

U

United Nations (UN), 28, 37–38, 48–50, 56–57, 59–60, 66–75, 81–85, 94–96, 141, 153–157, 161
urban design, 153–157

V

Van der Linden, Sander, 104–108
Vogler, John, 73–76

Y

Yasseri, Taha, 158–161